Creative
LIVING ROOM
DECORATING

Cover pictures: (top) IPC Magazines/Robert
Harding Syndication; (bl) IPC Magazines/Robert
Harding Syndication; (br) Casablanca range of
fabrics from Harlequin Fabrics & Wallcoverings,
Cossington Road, Sileby, Leicestershire, LA12
7RU, UK. Tel: 01509 816575.

Page 1: Elizabeth Whiting & Associates/Nadia
McKenzie; Page 3: Elizabeth Whiting &
Associates/Spike Powell; Page 4: Eaglemoss/
Graham Rae; Page 5: Eaglemoss/Graham Rae.

First published in North America
in 1996 by Betterway Books,
an imprint of F&W Publications Inc.,
1507 Dana Avenue,
Cincinnati, Ohio 45207
1-800/289-0963

ISBN 1-55870-416-7

Manufactured in Hong Kong

10 9 8 7 6 5 4 3 2 1

CREATING YOUR HOME

Creative
LIVING ROOM
DECORATING

BETTERWAY BOOKS

Contents

INSPIRATIONS
Create a mood, color scheme and style

ESSENTIALS
Plan the lay-out, seating and storage

ACCESSORIES
Make your own finishing touches

CREATING A MOOD BOARD

Visualizing the mood you want a room to have before you start redecorating means that you can create a special sense of identity for it that reflects your personality while catering to your needs.

W hether you're starting from scratch or trying to breathe new life into a dull room, taking that first step can be intimidating. You probably have some basic ideas, perhaps you'd like to try a country motif, or you want to match new additions to existing furniture, but how do you turn your vision into reality?

You can bridge the image gap by compiling a mood board from a selection of pictures and bric-a-brac that make you feel good. If you enjoy the outdoor life, for instance, you probably find country or seaside scenes enticing; on the other hand, if you are inspired by art and architecture, you may find old portraits or stately interiors generate loads of ideas. The object of the exercise is to concentrate your mind on personal penchants for certain colours, textures and moods, and thereby establish the basis of an appealing look for the room.

Initially, the aims of a mood board may seem somewhat removed from the reality of decorating a room. Yet the concept is similar to when you look at a picture of a tropical island with bleached coral sand and green palm trees set in a sparkling blue sea and think how lovely it would be to live in such idyllic surroundings. A mood board is a step towards incorporating a feeling of tropical bliss – or another atmosphere of your choice – into your own surroundings.

The inspiration for a design scheme often lies close to home. In this airy cottage living room, a glance out of the window quickly accounts for the choice of a country-fresh green and white colour scheme that is as crisp and sharp as green apples after a shower of rain.

COLLECTING INSPIRATION

When it comes to seeking guidance and motivation for any particular design direction, a pile of magazines and newspapers is a treasure trove of ideas. Basically you want to look out for pictures with a special gasp factor, that literally take your breath away with their phenomenal beauty or drama and that you feel you would like to live with in your home in some form or another.

A good place to start is to build up a collection of magazines that you are prepared to cut up. While interior design magazines are naturally a useful source of ideas, all sorts of images are fuel for a fertile imagination – advertisements and sheet music, for instance, can equally well spur your creativity.

Flick through the magazines and tear or cut out anything that attracts your attention. It won't necessarily be related to interiors; it may be a bright pink fluffy sweater, a picture of a drystone wall or a Roman mosaic – literally anything that conveys a feel of the way you want the room to look. If you do fancy a warm scheme using pinks and reds, for instance, in addition to the pink sweater, a picture

of a glowing sunset might contain all the colours you want to incorporate, and suggest a cool mauve-grey in the night sky as background to the warmer colours.

There's no need to restrict yourself to photographs and prints; you only have to look at the colours, patterns and textures in nature and fashion to get plenty of marvellous ideas. You can collect bits and pieces from country walks, do a spot of beachcombing or find a few antique buttons at a garage/boot sale. Anything that catches your eye has potential for stirring your imagination.

You may be lucky and find a picture that hits the design nail right on the head, but it is unusual for one particular image to embody the essence of the room you have in your mind's eye. A mood board is likely to be a collage of different pictures and oddments. The process of putting it together is a practical, hands-on way of developing your impressions about the way the room might look. It provides an opportunity to express your feelings and ideas in terms of colours, shapes and textures and to think about interpreting the images in a decorative manner.

▲ *Starting from scratch*
Faced with bare walls and boards plus un-upholstered furniture, you need to find a sense of direction for the room. In this instance, it's easy to understand how a few mouthwatering images of vibrant blue and white scenery, plants and objects supply the impetus for the whole room scheme.

▶ *A powerful incentive*
Who, for example, could resist the magnificence of the dazzling white wedding-cake steeple and cobalt blue dome against the purest azure sky and not wish to live with a similar colour scheme?

◀ *Catching the mood*

*Translated into interior design reality, the
froth of the surf in the moonlight becomes
the sheer curtains; the detail on the blue and
white Delft tiles appears in the patterns on
the blind, rug, upholstery, lampshade and
china plates; the foliage of the blue flowers
points up the value of green as relief in an
exclusively blue and white, Scandinavian-
type scheme.*

CREATING A COLLAGE

From your collection of images, you are aiming to create a pleasing collage of colours and textures – not a representation of the room itself. You need a piece of cardboard large enough to accommodate an arrangement of all your cuttings and inspirational oddments.

Arrange and rearrange the cuttings on the board to see how they influence each other. Cut out parts of pictures or shapes in outline and superimpose some and leave others in isolation. You may find some ideas seem to point in the same direction while others don't fit in. Now is the time to discard and add as you please. If you have enough material and find it taking you in several directions, you can lay out two or three alternative boards for the same room, to offer yourself and your family a choice.

At this point, you should position your finished mood board somewhere in the room you are redecorating – or elsewhere in the house if that room is not in frequent use – to familiarize yourself with the general impression and reassure yourself that you are happy with where your choice is leading so far.

Combined with a list of practical requirements, the mood board acts as a valuable reference point for the next stage in the decorating process – that of selecting actual swatches and pattern samples for decorating the room. A finished mood board is there to endorse your personal choice of colour scheme and style for the room.

▲ Natural resources

The multiplicity of earthy colours and rough textures in natural materials and craftwork is very stimulating. You can see how the range of neutral and brownish colours in the baskets of beans and grains at an African market reappear in a charmingly decorated living room. Stone walls, spices and wickerwork inspire the details, while the glazed interiors of the terracotta urns are a reminder of the contrast value of shiny surfaces among roughened or matt ones – put into practice in the dark, polished wooden furniture in the room.

COORDINATED OPTIONS

Take the guesswork out of creating a colour scheme by mixing and matching fabrics, wallcoverings, paints and accessories from a fully coordinated design package.

The most recent coordinating ranges cover every decorating eventuality, from the basics such as fabrics, wallpaper, paint and tiles to accessories like bedlinen and lampshades. Many carry coordination through to the finest details of matching ceramics and tea-towels.

A fully integrated package of plains and patterns offers an enormous range of decorative possibilities. There are several decorating strategies you can adopt. You can go all out for creating a total look, using as many elements as you deem necessary from the same coordinated range to achieve a completely matched finish. Alternatively, you can take a more selective approach, omitting entire pattern themes or changing the proportions of the patterns used in the scheme to tilt the balance towards a particular style.

The sample range in the room schemes that follow is representative of many coordinated collections and is used to illustrate the adaptability of coordinating ranges in general. It offers a strong signature or master floral pattern that carries a visual index of all the colours in the rest of the range. Such a dominant design usually features as a fabric with matching wallpaper and complementary border design. Depending on the amount you use, it serves either as an eye-catching mainstay or a universal link in the scheme.

Typical supplements to the main pattern are colour-matched geometrics or plains: in this case a checked fabric, striped wallpaper and a deep pink textured fabric. Paint in two shades of pink and a neutral beige is also used. The floral design is picked out again in ready-made accessories like a blind and stationery.

The signature floral of a coordinating range holds centre stage at the window, while the floral border and cushions disperse the traditional theme round the room. Colour-linked, low-key checks and pink walls soften the forceful floral pattern.

GOING BY THE BOOK

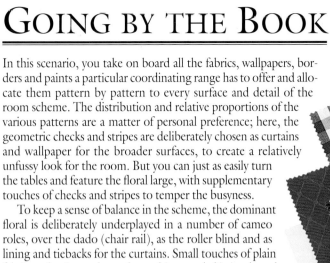

In this scenario, you take on board all the fabrics, wallpapers, borders and paints a particular coordinating range has to offer and allocate them pattern by pattern to every surface and detail of the room scheme. The distribution and relative proportions of the various patterns are a matter of personal preference; here, the geometric checks and stripes are deliberately chosen as curtains and wallpaper for the broader surfaces, to create a relatively unfussy look for the room. But you can just as easily turn the tables and feature the floral large, with supplementary touches of checks and stripes to temper the busyness.

To keep a sense of balance in the scheme, the dominant floral is deliberately underplayed in a number of cameo roles, over the dado (chair rail), as the roller blind and as lining and tiebacks for the curtains. Small touches of plain fabric and paintwork on the cushions and skirting boards perform a significant part in anchoring the mixture of patterns. The dark pink skirting grounds the strongly patterned dado, while the matching cushions add an essential colour accent to the green-checked armchair.

◨ *Within the range*
An astounding variety of different looks is possible using 11 basic elements from a coordinating range. All the room schemes illustrated in this feature are put together from a classic combination of a floral and striped wallpaper, a complementary floral border, a luscious floral fabric, two tones of green check and wine-coloured fabrics plus deep pink, pale pink and cream paints set against a green carpet.

◧ *Establishing a total look*
By definition, all the elements of a coordinating range are compatible. How ever you mix and match the allied designs and accessories you are bound to end up with a harmonious scheme. But in your use of the patterns you can tilt the outcome towards a specific look. In this room, for example, by favouring a predominance of checks and stripes and casting the flamboyant floral in supporting roles, you end up with a well worked out designer look for the room.

◪ *Fine tuning*
To go with many coordinating collections there is a range of ready-made accessories to match, from lampshades, tiebacks and picture frames to covered boxes, note books and soft toys. For the ultimate in continuity, some include a choice of colour-coordinated picture mounts to tie in with the patterns.

BEING SELECTIVE

Although manufacturers present a long and appetizing menu of coordinated designs in their pattern books, you are under no compulsion to include a bit of everything in one range in your scheme. You can achieve equally unified decorations by picking and choosing just one or two fabrics, a wallpaper and a few details from the range. Such a self-censoring approach to pattern selection can make decorating simpler, especially for novice designers.

You can make your personal selection on the basis of colour or pattern, or both, following a thematic or geometric path. In this version of the room scheme, the green checked fabric is omitted altogether in favour of a dominant floral for the curtains and upholstery and a striped paper on the walls.

Leaving out the green checked pattern definitely tips the colour balance towards the pinkness in the floral. The direction of the colour theme is further reinforced by a deep pink skirting, the pink cushions and matching covered footstool. Without a border at picture or dado rail level, or any change of pace over the dado area itself, the overall image is one of warm, restrained elegance.

◪ Comprehensively floral

For all-over styling, it is very useful to have a matching fabric and wallpaper in the range. Opting for a purely floral scheme, and swapping the pink striped wallpaper for the floral one with a matching border and deep pink wall above, points the room towards a rich Victorian style.

⬛ Lightening the mood
Cutting the striped wallpaper down to dado level, topping it off with the floral border and painting the rest of the wall pale pink and the skirting cream immediately serves to freshen and modernize the overall scheme.

◧ Creating a specific look
With an emphasis on the showy floral fabric and refined pink stripe wallpaper, here the room emerges with a quietly romantic feel. The floral curtains are draped softly to echo the curvy motifs on the fabric and the rounded shape of the armchair. Holding full-length curtains back high up like this accentuates the height of the window, reinforcing the effect of the striped walls.

15

REDIRECTING A LOOK

There are no hard and fast rules on how you should deploy the various elements of a coordinating range in a scheme. The designer of the package takes all the guesswork out of colour and pattern matching, virtually guaranteeing a harmonious scheme, while you reap all the compliments for the arrangement. It's up to you in what proportions and where you position the designs in the room. You can follow many style directions, depending on the colours and designs you favour.

▶ *The other way round*

A reversal of the fabric placements in the opening look for the room demonstrates how effectively you can transform the image of a room, even when using identical designs. In moving the patterns around, the proportion and prominence of the checked fabric at the window increase, conveying a more contemporary image. The deeper pink on the walls and the contrast check cushions on the floral-upholstered armchair are consistent with this bolder, up-to-date approach.

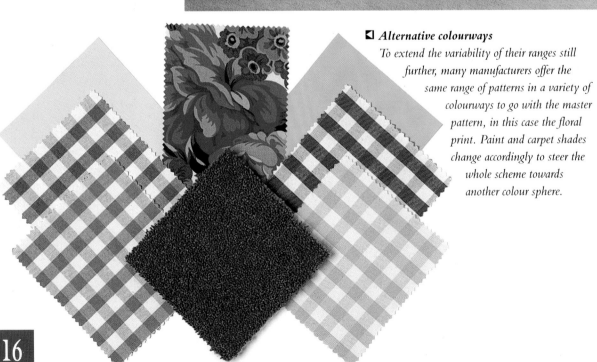

◀ *Alternative colourways*

To extend the variability of their ranges still further, many manufacturers offer the same range of patterns in a variety of colourways to go with the master pattern, in this case the floral print. Paint and carpet shades change accordingly to steer the whole scheme towards another colour sphere.

COTTAGE LIVING ROOMS

Warm and inviting, the cottage living room provides a peaceful refuge from the pressures of modern life. With its pretty chintzes and cosy furnishings, it's like a breath of fresh country air.

Traditional yet informal, the country cottage style provides a sympathetic, welcoming setting for relaxation and family life. Materials are natural and robust enough to take a little wear and tear, patterns and colours evoke the freshness and beauty of the countryside. There's room for old favourites, too – cherished heirlooms and mementoes, such as framed samplers, patchwork and tapestry cushions, sit well in this comfortable blend.

You don't need a view of rolling hills or a period home to recreate the look. Even the most urban of locations is transformed with the right furnishings and accessories into a haven of country charm. The traditional cottage is small in scale and relatively simple in terms of architectural detailing, and elements of this ever-popular look are readily available and affordable. What better environment to unwind in and escape from the hustle-bustle of busy city life?

Painted brick walls and exposed beams, a leafy rug laid over wooden floorboards and a burst of floral chintz on upholstery, cushions and curtains make this living room the epitomy of fresh and cosy country cottage style.

17

SETTING THE SCENE

Walls In the cottage style, wall treatments are simple and pretty – there's no need to make a grand statement with strong colour or refined detail. Plain whitewash over rough plasterwork has a rugged charm; for a richer background opt for terracotta, soft peach or cream washed on in loose strokes. Simple broken colour effects, using two or more tones of the same shade, give depth and character to modern walls.

If you prefer the more enveloping look, choose a small-scale floral or leaf print in fresh, light colours. You can paper the wall from floor to ceiling or stop two-thirds of the way down and cover the dado (chair rail) with painted tongue-and-groove boarding. For extra definition, edge the walls with a matching paper border. You can also introduce pattern with stencilling – ideal if you enjoy the hand-finished look. Trailing designs of leaves and vines, or small flower sprigs in soft pastels evoke the country mood.

Ceilings Extending colour over the ceiling helps to make a room feel more enclosed. For a whole-hearted country look, apply beams to the ceiling – stain them black, leave them natural or paint them to match the ceiling finish.

Floors Natural flooring provides a sympathetic base to the look. Exposed floorboards, stripped, waxed to a soft honey colour or stained a dark oak shade, are comfortable underfoot and easy to maintain. Carpeting in a solid neutral shade complements country decor – or investigate the possibilities of natural fibre coverings such as sisal, coir and seagrass. Old cottages often boast stone flagged or brick floors. You can achieve a similar effect with terracotta tiling, although this may prove rather chilly for modern tastes.

Whatever style of flooring you choose, add instant colour and pattern with scatter rugs in homespun designs. Cheerful rag rugs, and hand-made hooked or needlepoint rugs in floral patterns add both comfort and interest.

Fireplace The cosy focus of the cottage parlour is the fireplace. Country hearths are typically wide and finished in rustic materials. Oak mantel beams, exposed stone or brickwork chimney breasts and simple iron firebaskets for burning logs have a look of rugged simplicity. If you wish to transform an existing fireplace, choose a simple wooden or stone surround rather than a fancier period style. Generous wicker log baskets and wrought iron or polished brass fireplace accessories complete the picture.

Windows Cottage windows are typically small and deepset, often with small leaded panes. Not every home boasts such features, but you can reduce the apparent size of a large window by covering it with a deep ruched blind. Keep curtains pretty and unfussy, with simple gathered headings and shaped fabric tiebacks. For an intimate look, coordinate curtains with upholstery. Lace panels partnered with print curtains look charming and filter the light in a pleasing way.

ELEMENTS OF THE STYLE

The cosy atmosphere of this room is typical of the cottage look. The main features are pinpointed below to help you achieve the same effect in your living room. Look at the pictures on the following pages for more ideas.

WALLS AND CEILING

Buttermilk paint on the walls is carried over to the ceiling, creating a restful backdrop and giving the room a cosy, intimate atmosphere. Rustic wooden beams are left exposed.

SEATING

A rush-seated wooden chair supplements the easy chair and sofa, upholstered in a plain cotton weave; chintz would make a fresh and pretty alternative.

FIREPLACE

A wide fireplace with a brick hearth and brass club fender is the focal point of the room, with all the seating arranged around it. A basket of logs is kept close at hand next to the hearth, while the fire irons are propped up against a large log at the front.

STORAGE AND ACCESSORIES

Recess shelving makes a good spot to display chunky crockery and to store a well-thumbed collection of books. Daintier ornaments are perched along the sash-window ledge, bordered with framed photographs on the bay walls. Botanical prints and pictures break up the wall space and flowers add freshness.

WINDOW

The deep bay window is fitted with a window seat, complete with pretty floral cushions, including a stencilled one, and plenty of interesting ornaments and prints to supplement the view outside. Roller blinds fixed against the windows provide instant shade. The floral curtains frame the bay window when they are open and insulate the room when they are drawn closed.

FLOORS

A patterned wool rug laid over a plain, neutral-coloured carpet adds a dash of colour and extra comfort underfoot.

COTTAGE FURNISHINGS

Cottages are modest in size, so it is important to keep furnishings on a suitably small scale. Group seating around the fireplace, with small occasional tables conveniently at hand for holding lamps and ornaments.

Seating Traditional-style wing armchairs and comfortable sofas are classic country pieces. Avoid the coordinated look of the three-piece suite – a small two-seater sofa and a pair of armchairs makes a more flexible arrangement. Leather club chairs, traditional Windsor chairs or ladderbacks also strike the right note of country informality. For a lighter countrified effect, opt for cane or wickerwork conservatory furniture.

Cottage-style alternatives to the modern coffee table are an old wooden trunk or blanket box – also excellent for storage – or a low ottoman or upholstered stool. Side tables in dark polished timber, pine or wickerwork are useful accessories.

Upholstery Pretty floral chintz is the essential country fabric. Chairs and sofas covered in chintz loose covers make inviting places to curl up with a good book. Needlepoint seat or cushion covers add another layer of pattern. Nubbly linen, plain calico and strong cotton blends are ideal for all-purpose upholstery. Add warm woollen throws and blankets or paisley shawls to soften the lines of the furniture and provide colour accents.

Lighting Lighting is an important element in creating the cosy ambience of the cottage living room. A selection of small table lamps with porcelain or ceramic bases and fabric or pleated paper shades create glowing points of light around the room. Wall-mounted sconces with individual candle shades or a central pendent light of a similar design are also in keeping with the look. Painted or frosted glass shades give out a warm, flattering light. Standard lamps positioned behind chairs provide a good level of illumination for reading or sewing.

Storage Hide the accessories of modern living from view in old pine chests, wooden chests-of-drawers or corner cupboards. Cottage-style storage furniture is refreshed by stripping away old varnish and paint and stencilling a pretty design on doors or drawer fronts.

 Simple tastes

If chintz is not to your taste, create a country-style interior with natural, homespun fabrics in soft beiges and creams. Warm-toned wooden and wicker furniture set against plain painted walls, and floorboards topped with natural matting, create a restful scheme.

▶ *Country seat*

Dainty flowers and trailing leaves abound in this cosy corner – on the mix-and-match chintz cushions on the window seat, the floral rug, sweeping curtain and matching foliate wallpaper – not forgetting the genuine article spilling out from a large glass vase.

◄ Peaceful retreat
In this contemporary interpretation of cottage style, duck-egg blue walls create a fresh backdrop for chintz-covered sofas and country-style wooden furniture, including a country dresser and old-fashioned rocker. Natural matting is the preferred choice of flooring for this modern cottage look.

▼ Natural evolution
The cottage look is one that evolves over the years, resulting in a homely mixture of furnishings – like the mismatched fabrics of this table cloth, sofa, cushion and curtains, and the wide range of accessories, each with its story to tell.

21

Seek out examples of traditional country craftwork to accessorize your cottage living room, and bring nature indoors with lush, informal posies or baskets of flowers and foliage.

◤ Sample of the country
Pieces of traditional country craftwork, like these embroidered samplers and cushions, add a homely, lived-in air to the room. They're a pleasure to collect or to embroider yourself.

◤ Cushy number
A Windsor chair is given the soft treatment with a cheerful patchwork cushion. The window treatment, with its simple floral curtains and lace frill, is pure country.

▷ From the garden
A pot of winter heather and a jug of anemones add an invigorating dash of country colour. Small occasional tables like this one are perfect for the look.

AMERICAN HERITAGE LIVING ROOM

The American heritage-style living room is inspired by the natural materials and homespun flavour of early America, combined with today's rich colours and comfy furniture.

The appeal of the American heritage-style living room extends far beyond national boundaries. Blending clean lines and functional design with rich earthy colours, warm-toned natural materials and folksy accessories, the style is orderly and uncluttered yet never sparse or impersonal.

Practicality, durability and informality are high priorities – traditional family life revolves around children, and their daily, rumbustious presence in the living room is taken for granted. Comfort is essential too – big, stuffed armchairs and sofas draped with American patchwork throws and clustered round the warmth of a

wood-burning fireplace are what good old-fashioned hospitality is all about.

Start by creating a backdrop of plain, pale or rich-toned walls, teamed with stripped pine boards, carpeting or natural matting on the floor. Though American heirlooms or antiques are helpful in furnishing the room, they're certainly not essential. Stripped, stained or polished wood furniture of a simple, classic design is fine, and you can clinch the style with well chosen accessories. Handcrafted, old-fashioned toys, samplers, patchwork cushions and throws, rag rugs and folk paintings and prints are all typical, reflecting the American love of nostalgia.

Cream-painted, vertical tongue-and-groove boarding and a comfortable armchair upholstered in chalky blue and white stripes typify the simple charm of American heritage style. Well designed, open storage space doubles as a display case for handsome domestic items such as these Shaker-style and turned-wood boxes.

CREATING THE LOOK

Walls In a small room, paint or paper the walls in cream or white and pick out woodwork in strong, flat colours – teal or indigo-blue, hunter green, grey-green, yellow-ochre, charcoal grey and burgundy are all typical. Continuing a pale wall colour over the ceiling creates a sense of spaciousness. In a larger room, paint all the walls in one of these shades, with richly contrasting trims.

Use vertical or horizontal tongue-and-groove boarding or matchboarding as a dado or floor-to-ceiling finish. It can be custom-built or in self-assembled panels, and left natural or painted or stained in suitable colours. Alternatively, use a white or pale wallpaper that's striped to resemble vertical matchboarding, or paint your own stripes and shadows for a trompe l'oeil effect.

Simple, decorative motifs stencilled on plain walls are quintessentially American. Stencil motifs at picture rail or cornice height, around door and window frames, or evenly spaced all over for a wallpaper-like effect.

Picture rails, Shaker-style peg rails and dado rails divide up panelling, wallpaper and painted surfaces for a richly contrasting effect.

Floors Go for stripped or stained, narrow or wide pine floorboards with rag or other scatter rugs added. Stencil a border round the edge of a wooden floor to add a folksy touch. Plain or floral-patterned fitted carpet in neutral or rich tones, natural-fibre floorcovering and quarry tiles are also suitable.

Windows Sash windows are ideal, unadorned if privacy allows or fitted with simple blinds or with sill or floor-length curtains hung from brass or iron rods, slender wooden poles or Shaker-style peg rails. Fit deep windowsills with comfortable cushions. Gingham, hessian, calico, muslin and mattress ticking are authentic, practical and inexpensive fabric choices for window dressings.

Lighting Electrical, wrought-iron chandeliers, hung from a central ceiling rose, and electrical, wall-hung candle holders of wrought iron or pressed tin are ideal for the look. Freestanding glass lamps, such as opaque milk glass or cranberry glass, and old-fashioned oil lamps create the right mood. Lamp bases made from stencilled, weighted metal canisters, hand-painted metal toleware or salt-glazed storage jars make authentic-looking accessories.

ELEMENTS OF THE STYLE

This stylish interpretation of the American country-style living room, and the pictures on the following pages, contain many elements that you can introduce into an existing living room to give it an American country flavour.

WALLS AND CEILING

Walls painted a purple-blue, with detailing – including a Shaker peg rail – picked out in green make a colourful yet restful backdrop. Discreet built-in storage cupboards are painted to match the walls so as not to interfere with the smooth-flowing colour.

WINDOWS

The window frame and surround are painted green to match the scheme. A green-and-white striped blind is hung from a length of peg rail fixed over the window.

LIGHTING

White candles in a central, wrought-iron chandelier, wall sconces and mantelpiece candlesticks are authentic, but electric equivalents or simple brass or opaque glass bases, with opaque glass or fabric shades, are equally suitable.

FURNITURE

Mix and match American heritage-style wooden furniture with some comfortable upholstered pieces. Here, a sofa upholstered in a hardwearing plaid is teamed with a classic Windsor chair, spool-turned, polished wood side tables and little bench. Furniture is grouped around the painted, wooden fireplace – in green to match the other detailing.

ACCESSORIES

A few well chosen accessories – a flower-filled spongeware vase, a log basket, broom, model beehive and a simple sheep print – set the style without cluttering up the room.

FURNISHINGS

Furniture Traditional wooden furniture in a comfortable mix of classic styles is ideal for the look. The aim is to create the effect of family furniture handed down or collected from several sources. Simple Georgian, Victorian, Edwardian or even art nouveau originals or reproductions are suitable, together with timeless rural-style pieces, such as rocking chairs, settles and Windsor chairs. Avoid ornate, exotic or ultra-modern styles. Authentic woods include hickory, ash, maple, elm, pine, oak, mahogany and cherry, or you can use wood stains to mimic the look.

If you're on a tight budget, paint wicker or cane garden furniture white or rich, earthy colours and fit it with softening cushions. For comfortable seating, include an upholstered sofa, such as a Chesterfield or high-backed style with cabriole legs, and at least one upholstered chair, like a Chippendale-style wing chair. Circular-topped pedestal tables on tripod legs make ideal occasional tables.

Storage Heavy wooden chests, sideboards, cupboards and corner cupboards with open shelving above and covered shelving beneath are traditional. The wood can be scrubbed, stained, painted, varnished or stencilled. Sea chests and simple pine hope chests, in which young girls stored linen for their future married life, can be stencilled to match the decor, and double up as coffee tables. Contemporary matching fitted storage units aren't really in keeping with the look, but you can integrate them by painting them to match the walls and, if you wish, stencilling them with folksy motifs.

Smaller items of furniture such as bentwood chairs can be hung from Shaker-style peg rails when not in use. Shelves or stacks of Shaker-style lightweight wooden boxes, in a range of muted colours, have both storage and ornamental value.

Accessories Patchwork quilts and cushions in traditional American designs, such as log cabin, add a friendly touch; display a large quilt on a wall, drape it over a sofa or use it to disguise a table which doesn't quite fit in with the decor. Patchwork cushions add comfort to traditional high-backed wooden settles and rush-seated chairs, and a splash of colour to plain upholstered furniture.

Framed samplers provide a nostalgic touch; old originals are costly, but patterns based on them are available for stitching yourself, or you can create your own design to hand on down the generations.

Paintings and prints with simplified, childlike images and flattened perspective, are very much in keeping with the style. Folk art – old weathervanes, hand-made rag dolls or wooden carpenters' tools, for example – add a personal, finishing touch, whether as individual pieces or collections.

◧ *The American way*

Cream-painted, horizontal tongue-and-groove panelling with a finely stencilled frieze creates a neat background against which to set a mixed collection of furniture – a beech bentwood chair, oak milking stool and mahogany cabinet. Carved wooden decoy ducks and a patchwork cushion add an early American flavour, and a vase of fresh flowers is a softening influence.

◤ Creature comforts
In this inviting interpretation, comfort and the creation of a friendly, relaxed atmosphere are given priority. Upholstered seating in cotton fabrics is cosily grouped around a wooden coffee table. Fresh flowers and plants and plenty of handcrafted accessories provide points of interest.

◥ Reader's refuge
Burgundy and hunter green are classic colours for the look. In this snug reading corner, the red-and-white checked chair and patchwork cushion look twice as inviting set against the muted backdrop.

◤ Sitting pretty
A comfortable mix of furniture styles gives this living room its homey, lived-in feel. Here a ladderback, rush-seated rocking chair in dark, polished wood is teamed with upholstered armchairs and an unusual coffee table made from a cut-down butcher's block.

DETAILS

Accessorize your living room with humble but handsome old-fashioned domestic objects and handcrafted items, such as wooden trinket boxes, old tin lanterns and patchwork cushions. Keep displays simple and orderly and avoid clutter at all costs. Punctuate walls with framed samplers and folk prints and paintings.

◄ *Illuminating*
Wall-hung, pressed tin candleholders in simple geometric shapes combine the practical with the decorative in true American heritage style.

◄ *Red, white and blue*
Fly the flag with furnishings and accessories in all-American red, white and blue. Here, remnants of checked furnishing fabrics are used to create decorative padded hearts, globes and a duck, reminiscent of old-fashioned nursery toys.

▲ *Off the peg*
Use a painted, Shaker-style hanging rail, made of short lengths of dowel inserted at regular intervals into a batten, to support curtains as well as pictures.

◄ *Timeless style*
Old-fashioned wooden clocks in matt-finished, earthy tones have a solid, reliable feel that's ideal for the look.

▶ *Rags to riches*
Woven out of fabric remnants, circular or oval rag rugs add a truly authentic touch.

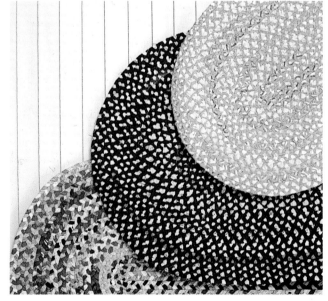

SCANDINAVIAN LIVING ROOMS

Scandinavian style, with its wide, uncluttered spaces, blond wood and pale paint finishes, makes for an airy and refined decor that strikes the perfect balance between comfort and elegance.

In the northern countries that make up Scandinavia – Sweden, Norway, Denmark and Finland – where winters are long and dark, there is a natural tendency to make the most of the precious hours of daylight. In the traditional Scandinavian-style home, colour, decoration and even furniture arrangement all collaborate to enhance whatever natural light a room receives. The result is a fresh, uncluttered and elegant decor with an air of peaceful harmony – what better decorating style for a living room where you while away your leisure time?

The Scandinavian style as we know it today has its roots in the eighteenth century and the reign of King Gustav III of Sweden – hence the term 'Gustavian' used to describe grander interpretations of the look. Gustavian style is formal and classical, but never overbearing or pretentious. Elegant wooden furniture with billowing lines and decorative carvings, gilded mirrors, rococo chandeliers and fine porcelain are set against walls washed with pearly grey-blue or pale green. In its more countrified version, Scandinavian style includes homespun weaves, soft clear colours and natural finishes, teamed with more functional yet still elegant furniture and simple artifacts, such as tin lanterns, iron candlesticks and rag runners.

However you interpret the look, the emphasis on light and the sense of restraint create naturally harmonious and comfortable rooms which are the perfect antidote to the hustle and bustle of modern day living.

A mood of faded elegance permeates this Gustavian-style living room. Watery green paintwork and stone-coloured walls with discreet stencilling make a harmonious backdrop for refined eighteenth-century furniture and a magnificent Scandinavian tiled stove. Simple checked upholstery and bare floorboards bring the style down to earth.

CREATING THE LOOK

Walls Paint is the essential finish for Scandinavian-style backgrounds. For an elegantly neo-classical look, walls can be painted in smooth matt chalky shades of stoney white, pale straw, soft grey-blue or watery green, and mouldings discreetly picked out with touches of gilding. These subtle neutrals and paler colours from the cool end of the spectrum heighten the effect of natural light. Mid-blue and luminous aquamarine also work well if you prefer stronger shades.

Slightly distressed finishes created by colour-washing or glazing add depth and character. More overt patterning can be achieved with a specialist paint effect, like dragging or marbling – keep the colours soft and muted. Add interest to plain painted walls with simple stencilled motifs or apply strips of profiled beading to suggest panelling. Plaster or synthetic mouldings, such as ceiling roses, add a grand flourish; they're widely available and relatively easy to install – choose the simpler, classical designs for a more authentic look and enrich with gilding if you desire.

Floors A sweeping expanse of bare floorboards is a defining feature of the look. Scrubbed, sanded and lightly waxed, the homey quality of the boards provides a forthright contrast to the elegance of furnishings. Timber floors in older houses are usually in pine. You can make the old boards good by stripping and sanding, then sealing them. However, the standard orangey colour of sealed pine is somewhat at odds with the cooler colours of Scandinavian decor; if necessary you can lighten the tone of pine by applying a liming paste or bleach solution, or rub white paint well into the grain before finishing. Seal the boards with matt varnish or wax.

Rag runners, made of strips of bright cloth remnants, are highly evocative of Scandinavian style. Traditionally a long runner was placed around the perimeter of the room to form a carpeted walkway and protect the floor from wear.

Windows Treat windows simply to maximize the amount of light flooding into the room. A wisp of muslin looped over a pole or tied up in loose knots to form a pelmet (cornice) softens the lines of a window without sacrificing daylight. Simple gingham or ticking curtains, caught back high up to provide an Empire-line profile, give more privacy; or fit windows with panelled wooden shutters, painted to tone with the walls.

Lighting For a grand Gustavian flourish, opt for gilded, mirrored wall sconces, ornate silver candlesticks and an extravagant rococo chandelier. For a humbler interpretation of the style, tin lanterns, pierced metal wall sconces and plain iron candlesticks all have Scandinavian charm. Or you can play up the look's contemporary appeal with modern-style table and standing lamps – choose models with clean, unfussy lines and add plain cream or simple checked shades.

ELEMENTS OF THE LOOK

This contemporary interpretation of the look contains all the basic elements of Scandinavian style – spaciousness, simplicity and restrained elegance. Look to the features pinpointed here and the pictures on the following pages to recreate the effect in your home.

WALLS

Walls are painted stoney white, with the colour continued on to the window frames and pelmet boxes, opening out the room and creating a sense of light and space. For a grander effect, use soft grey-blue, pale straw or pale green, and add interest with gilded mouldings.

FLOOR

Bleached floorboards are a typical Scandinavian feature. A blue and white checked rug adds warmth and comfort.

FURNITURE

Contemporary furniture with clean lines and in pale wood, upholstered in plain, checked or printed cotton, sits well in a simple Scandinavian-style decor. For a grander, Gustavian look, opt for elegant eighteenth-century, French-style pieces with billowing lines and decorative carvings, painted in delicate hues with touches of gilding.

LIGHTING

Old and new styles of lighting are combined – a gilded wall sconce with three curving arms bearing dainty candlelamps gives atmospheric background lighting, supplemented by a modern-look table lamp.

WINDOWS

Pelmet boxes (cornices) with flowing serpentine edges add a flourish to the windows, but are painted white to keep the look understated. Straightforward floor-length drapes in a crisp cotton print add a welcome colour accent and echo the blue and white china theme – they draw right back to let in maximum light.

ACCESSORIES

Blue and white china vases, pots and ginger jars are inexpensive to buy and perfect for the look. Here they pick up on the blue and white theme of the soft furnishings. Plaster ceiling roses painted white and mounted on the wall create a classical display. A tall glass vase of white lilies adds freshness.

FURNISHINGS

Furniture The key to the look is keeping the room relatively sparsely furnished, with plenty of clear floor space. Push furniture back against the walls to free up maximum space. Scandinavian-style furniture displays good clean lines and painted finishes, often in white or clear colours. The design of such pieces is basically classical; chairs may have tapering legs and oval backs, sofas may be in the form of Greek-style couches. Some modern retailers now produce good versions of such pieces, which are soundly constructed and affordable.

Traditionally, furniture which was made of pine was generally painted. Appropriate colours are delicate and pale – the same blue-greens, grey-blues and off-whites evident on the walls. Mouldings or carved detail may be enhanced with a little gilding.

Upholstery on chair seats, couches and sofas has a surprisingly homespun quality. Ticking, gingham and calico are typical of the style. Tie-on cushions soften the seats of chairs; alternatively chair seats may be cane. Benches or upright sofas can be upholstered with long buttoned gusset cushions like thin mattresses; additional cushions come in the form of neat, tailored bolsters.

Accessories Details bring the style into focus and create the right look of understated grandeur. But it's important to exercise a sense of restraint: cluttered arrangements of accessories quickly detract from the overall simplicity and refinement of the style.

Gilt, glass and mirror provide reflective surfaces to contrast with the pale, matt textures of surfaces and furnishings. A classical mirror with a carved and gilded frame makes an elegant statement. Mirrored wall sconces arranged in symmetrical pairs multiply the effect of light, while a central crystal chandelier creates a glittering focus of interest. Other sympathetic accessories include silver candlesticks, Chinese porcelain or crystal bowls.

A less formal version of the style can be suggested with simpler artifacts such as tin lanterns and pierced metal wall sconces, pewter jugs and plain iron candlesticks.

◤ *Capture the look*

A gilt-framed engraving hung on a stone-coloured wall with fine stencilled detailing, a humble candleholder and hurricane lamp, and two fabric-covered antique books laid on a handsomely carved, painted and gilded wooden side table – all strike the right note of understated elegance that typifies the Scandinavian style.

◣ *A comfortable mix*

Blend the aspects of Scandinavian style that you most admire with elements from other looks to create a decor perfectly tailored to your needs. Here an essentially Scandinavian-style living room – light and airy with plain white walls, simple furnishings and bare floorboards – is given a friendlier, lived-in look by the squashy sofa and heavier accessorizing.

◢ Old meets new

Although Gustavian style dates back to the eighteenth century, the essential feeling of spaciousness and simplicity is wholly in keeping with modern tastes. Here traditional and contemporary styles come together in the choice of furniture and accessories – all shown off to advantage against a backdrop of plain white painted walls and handsome parquet flooring, flooded with natural light.

◢ Rhapsody in blue

Soft grey-blues are a trademark feature of the Scandinavian look, creating elegant and restful schemes ideally suited to living rooms. They're used throughout this room, on the simple two-colour fabrics of the curtains, bench cushions and chair upholstery, on the painted bench and even the natural matting floorcovering, set against a background of cool grey walls.

DETAILS

The Scandinavian style is uncluttered, airy and spacious, so keep accessories to a minimum – whether you're recreating the splendour of a Gustavian-style interior or settling for a humbler or more contemporary interpretation.

◪ *A Gustavian flourish*
A splendid rococo-style silver candelabrum makes a sparkling addition to classic Scandinavian-style interiors.

◪ *Keep it simple*
Simple checks and printed cottons – in white and one other colour – work their magic in sparse Scandinavian-style settings. Rich red and dark green make a change from classic blue and white and are just as traditional.

◪ *Northern light*
This mirrored wall sconce with a gilded wooden frame is a copy of an original Gustavian design. The mirror reflects precious rays of sunlight during the day, and the glow of the candle flame at night.

◪ *Simply Scandinavian*
The crisp blue and white of the bowl, chair seat and rug are the perfect complement for the mellow tones of blond wood furniture.

VICTORIAN LIVING ROOMS

Charming and nostalgic, the Victorian-style living room makes an appealing focus for family life. If you're keen on the past, this is one of the easiest period looks to recreate in your home.

Besides being the place where visitors were entertained, the Victorian living room was a room which catered to a range of genteel family pursuits, from reading and sewing to parlour games and making music. With sympathetic ingredients, you can easily recapture the same cosy, homey mood. Original nineteenth century details, such as fireplaces and mouldings, undoubtedly help generate an authentic atmosphere. But even featureless modern rooms can be transformed by assembling the right furnishings, accessories and ornaments.

For an authentic Victorian look, fill the room with comfortable upholstered furniture, layers of drapery, potted plants and innumerable ornamental objects. Home-loving and sentimental, the Victorians always found a place to display their personal treasures and mementoes. Deep, warm colours, dense patterns, trimmings and exotic curios in a lively mixture of styles all serve to create a room with great depth and character.

A pretty frosted glass lamp casts a cosy glow over this comfortable room which is painted in warm apricot and carpeted throughout. The circular brass-topped table is covered with a typically Victorian collection of colourful scraps and cards.

SETTING THE SCENE

Walls and ceilings Pattern is the key to the Victorian interior. The secret of successful mixing is to select a range of designs which complement each other thematically and display the same basic family of colours.

Walls are generally sectioned into three distinct areas, subdivided by a picture rail about 30-45cm (12-18in) down from the ceiling, and a dado, which occupies the lower third of the wall surface. Cover the main wall area, between the picture rail and dado, with patterned wallpaper. The dado wallcovering should be more robust.

To recreate the Victorian effect, paper the middle section of the wall in a naturalistic design of flowers or leaves. Choose a dense, detailed print in soft, muted colours, such as sage green, olive, rose, russet, deep crimson, dull gold, cinnamon or chocolate brown. Many Victorian-style papers are available with matching borders and you can use these to mark the position of the dado, or apply a dado rail of ready-made moulding instead. The dado itself can be covered in a textured relief paper, painted in a toning shade.

Paint the ceiling in a warm off-white or cream. You can extend this colour down to the picture rail or fill the areas between the picture rail and ceiling with another patterned border for a richer effect. For a simplified version of the look, you can dispense with the dado and picture rails altogether.

Floors If you have a wooden floor, stain the boards dark brown and cover with a large pat-terned carpet or rug, leaving a narrow margin of floorboards exposed around the perimeter of the room. Alternatively, lay rugs over plain carpeting or fit wall-to-wall carpet in a design which blends sympathetically with the wallpaper. Large-scale floral designs are appropriate, as are Oriental patterns in glowing blues, reds and golds.

Woodwork Doors, skirting boards and all wooden trims should be painted or stained a dark wood colour. It is worth replacing modern flush doors with solid panelled versions which are more in keeping with the look. Alternatively, you could apply mitred wooden beading to create the effect of panelling on a plain door. Wooden panels for doors are available in kit form.

Architectural features No single architectural feature captures the look more effectively than a period fireplace. You can acquire an original nineteenth century fireplace from an architectural salvage company or fireplace specialist, or choose a suitable reproduction design. Plain white marble surrounds fitted with cast iron grates and painted cast iron fireplaces inset with bright tiled panels are the two most common forms. Dark wood fire surrounds are also appropriate.

Victorian sitting rooms often boasted decorative plasterwork cornices and ceiling roses. Modern reproductions are widely available in a variety of styles. Lightweight polystyrene mouldings are cheap, easy to install and, once painted, look almost as good as the real thing.

CREATING THE LOOK

The rich colours and ornamental detail of this room are typical of the Victorian style. Key features are pointed out to help you recreate the look in your own sitting room.

WALLS AND CEILING

The dark cream on the ceiling is extended down to picture rail level; below, the main part of the wall is covered with wallpaper in a leafy design in sage green and cream.

STORAGE

Choose glass-fronted dark wood cabinets which can be free-standing or wall-mounted. Here a writing table with drawer provides extra space for ornaments and mementoes.

ACCESSORIES

You can cover every surface with ornaments, including ornate candlesticks, photograph frames and lacquerwork items with an Oriental flavour.

FIREPLACE

The cast iron fireplace inset with decorative painted tiles is perfect for the period. Look for moulded wooden fire surrounds in home improvement stores.

FURNITURE

Comfortably upholstered armchairs complete with cushions are grouped around the fireplace. Dark wooden side tables provide a resting place for potted plants, bowls of fruit or vases of flowers.

VICTORIAN FURNISHINGS

Window treatments and drapery Dress windows in layers of fabric, lavishly trimmed for a sumptuous effect. Partner velvet outer curtains edged with fringing with delicate panels of lace, or combine floral printed cretonne with lightweight muslin drapery. Suspend curtains from a brass or dark wooden pole, or hide the heading behind a fabric-covered pelmet. Tie back the outer curtains with thick gold cord hooked over brass cleats.

The Victorian sitting room offers ample opportunity for other forms of drapery. Door curtains or portières, fringed table-cloths, lace runners and antimacassars – covers to protect the headrests of arm-chairs – give a soft, layered look.

Furniture and arrangement For maximum comfort, furniture should be grouped informally around the room with the fireplace as the principal focal point. A circular tripod table for taking tea, reading or writing letters might be the centrepiece of the arrangement. Combine deep cushioned armchairs and button-backed Chestefield sofas with occasional tables in polished mahogany.

Typically Victorian are balloon-back chairs, with round open backs and a padded seat, as well as more flamboyant gilt wood pieces inspired by French rococo and classical designs. There are plenty of good reproductions available, or you could update junk shop purchases with new upholstered coverings in floral prints, brocade, velvet or tapestry.

For an instant Victorian effect, layer sofas and chairs with paisley shawls, embroidered throws or kelim rugs, and pile with cushions. Leather club chairs and chaise longues work well with the style. To display all the accessories and ornaments that go with the look, choose glass-fronted cabinets or tiered stands ('what-nots'). Another essential is a large mirror over the mantelpiece. Victorian overmantle mirrors incorporate niches and shelves for showing off trinkets and knick-knacks.

Lighting It couldn't be easier to strike the right note with the vast range of reproduction table lamps and light fittings on the market. Table lamps with green glass shades and china or brass bases, wall-mounted etched or frosted glass globes on brass brackets, and central fixtures that hark back to the design of Victorian gasoliers are all widely available and eminently suitable.

▲ Plush warmth

A rich red and gold colour scheme and an abundance of velvet create a luxurious living room. Heavy curtains are lavishly trimmed with fringes and tassels while gilded picture frames and a two-armed chimney chandelier provide opulent details.

◄ A focal point

The white marble fireplace with an ornate gilt mirror above is typical of the Victorian style – look for good quality reproductions.

◄ Window dressing

The lavish festoons of an Austrian blind are teamed with an elegantly draped pair of fine sheers for a pretty effect at this window.

▼ On show

Every visible surface presents an opportunity for displaying favourite ornaments and knick-knacks.

Victorian homes were unashamedly cluttered, with any available surface used for arranging innumerable ornaments and accessories. Such a busy look – and the dusting – isn't for everyone, but if you enjoy collecting, this style offers the perfect excuse to put all your treasures on display.

Every Victorian table top and mantelpiece was crowded with exotic curios from far flung corners of the Empire, luxuriant potted palms and ferns, decorative objects from China and Japan, framed photographs, needlework panels and natural history specimens. Authentic accessories provide the essential finishing touch to a period room. Examples include standing screens with lacquerwork or tapestry panels, oval needlepoint firescreens, wax fruits under a glass dome, Oriental ceramics, papier mâché or lacquered boxes or peacock feathers in a vase.

◪ Colourful comfort
Handcrafted throws and cushion covers worked in strong colours brighten up a living room. Crochet, needlepoint and embroidery were all popular in the Victorian era.

◪ Cosy corner
Layers of rich fabric draped over tables and chairs give the room a comfortably upholstered feeling. Complete the look by grouping together personal mementoes and treasures and arranging them on side tables or the mantelpiece.

TOWN HOUSE LIVING ROOMS

Elegant and refined, the traditional town house style creates a sophisticated look that adapts happily to both modern and period homes at a surprisingly low cost.

The formal town house look is a natural choice for a living room, providing an elegant setting for some treasured possessions as well as a comfortable and restful place to relax. Gracefulness and a sense of spaciousness are the essential elements of this traditional look. High ceilings, large windows and architectural details give a room a good head start, but with a little know-how you can transform any room into a stylish living area that captures the elegance of times past.

Creating this smart yet comfortable image need not be costly – it might just be a case of making a few adjustments to the colour scheme and being imaginative with your choice of accessories or the arrangement of your existing furniture.

Plain, flat painted walls or unobtrusively patterned wallpapers help to create a sense of space, while classic shaped sofas and chairs upholstered in richly coloured and patterned fabrics give a warm, traditional feel. Elaborate curtain treatments add to the sense of period style, as do pieces of polished reproduction wooden furniture, or genuine antiques. This formal look is reinforced by suitable accessories such as pleated lampshades, gilded sconces, mirrors and picture frames.

A pale fawn and cream colour scheme brings this airy living room together. Period items such as straight-back upholstered chairs, a painted chest, fabric lampshades and precisely hung botanical prints create a stylish atmosphere.

CREATING THE STYLE

Walls Keep wall treatments unfussy – plain or papered walls in pale, classic background colours such as white or biscuit, lemon or pale dusky pink are best. These restful shades serve as subtle backdrops to rich colours and patterns in the furnishing fabrics. If you prefer patterned wallpaper choose one with a discreet regency stripe or tiny print, or perhaps an oriental-style (chinoiserie) design. Or you could put up wooden panelling over one or all walls. Once fixed, you can paint, stain or varnish the wooden panelling as desired.

Architectural details such as cornices and corbels highlighted in pure white provide interesting shapes and add style and grace. You could also add other decorative plaster features such as niches and ceiling roses – they are easy to put up and inexpensive to buy.

Often the fireplace is the focal point of the room. For an especially elegant style, a white marble surround is very effective, but a wooden fireplace, either stained or painted white, is also in keeping with the style. Woodwork should contrast with the walls and is usually painted white or ivory.

Floors Choose comfortable fitted carpets in discreet neutral colours to balance richly coloured upholstery fabrics. Alternatively, lay a large rug over polished floorboards. A large-scale design with a strong border, often in muted colours, is ideal.

Lighting Ceramic table lamps with empire or drum shades of pleated silk or chintz suit the style and provide localized, atmospheric lighting. If you want wall lamps choose plaster uplighters or gilded candle bracket-and-shade fittings.

Storage Fitted alcove shelving is ideal for books and ornaments. Alternatively position freestanding shelf units in a corner or along a wall so that they don't intrude into the room. Paint any fitted shelving or freestanding pine units white to match other woodwork and add decorative shelf trims for a traditional look.

Freestanding reproduction cabinets and bookcases are also useful for concealing incongruous technology, such as the television and stereo equipment. Inexpensive modern units with a dark wood veneer combine well with pieces of antique furniture.

ELEMENTS OF THE LOOK

Warmth and comfort, style and grace are essential elements of the town house living room. The most important features of the decorations, soft furnishings and furniture are pinpointed here to help you re-create the same feel in your own home. Look at the pictures on the following pages for different versions of the look.

WALLS

Plain pale colours and subtle stripes are ideal. Fresh white woodwork and architectural detailing contrast with the walls and add to the feeling of light and space throughout.

WINDOWS

For a formal look, traditional-style shutters painted white to match the rest of the woodwork are simple and effective, or choose elaborate drapes for a touch of warmth and luxury.

STORAGE

Blend fitted shelving by painting it to coordinate with the surrounding walls and woodwork.

FURNITURE

Comfortable easy chairs, often in different styles, are arranged formally around a focal point such as the fireplace or a coffee table. Upholstery and coordinating cushions usually incorporate a mixture of patterns and colours.

FLOOR

Wall-to-wall fitted carpet is warm and comfortable underfoot. Choose neutral colours which show off any upholstery and accessories in stronger colours.

ACCESSORIES

Gilt framed pictures of landscapes, portraits or botanical prints are just right for the look, as are flower arrangements and fine china.

Furniture A mixture of comfortable armchairs and sofas with antique or good reproduction pieces is formally arranged in a neat looking room. Upholstered furniture can be deliberately mismatched as long as you go for compatible styles such as wing chairs and open armchairs. Padded footstools look right as well.

Heavy and hardwearing upholstery brocades and velvet have an opulent feel, whether in neutral or strong vibrant colours. A cotton linen is a hardwearing, serviceable alternative. For a softer look, go for fresh chintz loose covers in light colours or pretty floral and leafy patterns to contrast with any dark wood furniture. Alternatively, try straightforward stripes, textured and plain shades to complement a highly patterned curtain fabric.

Other furniture is mainly polished mahogany, rosewood or walnut veneer in traditional styles. Age your existing furniture with a dark mahogany stain. Look in second-hand shops for armless, straight-backed upholstered chairs, and antique-style chests, writing desks and small side tables with turned legs and carved detail. If you can't find a suitable polished wood table, buy an MDF (medium density fibreboard), round, self-assembly one and cover it with a floor-length linen or damask cloth which harmonizes with the upholstery or curtain fabric.

Windows Curtain treatments are usually formal, even elaborate. Use generous amounts of fabric for very full, floor-length curtains. You can hold them back with coordinating fabric tiebacks or heavy cord and tassel tiebacks hooked on to shiny brass cleats.

A graceful fringed valance or pelmet is appropriate, or drape extra fabric into elaborate swags and tails over the top of the curtains. If you prefer a curtain pole, make it a heavy one in dark wood and use large wooden curtain rings. Flouncy Austrian blinds have a soft and charming appeal – they can be in matching or coordinating chintzes or plain glazed cottons.

Curtain fabrics are medium or heavyweight – choose large floral or leafy patterned chintzes if you want to match the curtains with loose chair covers and cushions. Choose damask for very fine, traditional style curtains or brocade for a grander, heavier look – brocade can also be used for upholstery and cushions.

▲ *Culture and society*
You can create a relaxed atmosphere with an inviting arrangement of comfortable classic furniture round an upholstered footstool. The white marble fireplace is an elegant focal point.

▶ *Additional pattern*
Draped side tables are an economical alternative, and offer the opportunity to introduce another pleasing pattern to the coordinated scheme.

◀ Neat ensemble
Elegant candlelamps and bunches of fresh flowers are fitting accessories for the town house look.

▶ Window dressing
Use ample amounts of leafy fabric for an extravagant swags-and-tails curtain treatment. Heavy cord and tassel tiebacks match the rich colour of the lining.

◢ Formal arrangements
Botanical prints help to reinforce a look of understated elegance. Carefully draped cords provide a link between theme pictures when they are arranged in a formal, balanced display like this.

THE FINER DETAILS

The town house living room is uncluttered and accessories few and well chosen. Select pieces whose designs hark back to the eighteenth century. A large carved and gilded mirror or family portrait looks imposing above the fireplace, while occasional tables are just the thing for displaying fine bone china, glass or silver.

◀ Touch of luxury
A heavy window drape in rich burgundy damask is tied back with a thick burgundy and gold cord for a luxurious touch.

▽ Finely crafted
An oval pedestal table in a rich, highly polished wood is ideal for a timeless town house living room.

▽ Establishing elegance
Carefully selected items set the style – look for table lamps with pleated fabric shades and classic furniture.

▽ Stylish veneer
A cherrywood veneer wall unit provides traditional-looking shelving that is ideal for displaying leather-bound books, classic ginger jars and other period-style objects.

SOFT MODERN LIVING ROOMS

*Welcoming and easy to live in, the soft
modern living room is practical to use and a pleasure
to look at as well.*

U p-to-date and unfussy, the soft modern look is essentially fresh and comfortable. The decorations and furniture are smart and elegant in a relaxed, friendly way that suits almost any type of lifestyle and home, whether it is old or new.

A sense of order and spaciousness is a basic feature of the softly modern approach. An expanse of plain flooring and a few pieces of simple furniture leave plenty of room to move round. Even in a smallish room, a feeling of space is achievable with pale colour scheming, the right lighting and furniture on a suitable scale.

Pastel colours, neutral shades or gentle patterns provide an easy-going background against which to introduce stronger colours in the soft furnishings. Rooms can also be livened up quickly and inexpensively with bright accent features like lamps, cushions, rugs and flowers, creating schemes of character and warmth.

The successful soft modern living room is refreshingly simple and user friendly. It relies on lively colour and pattern scheming, smart but comfy seating and plain furniture arranged in an orderly fashion for its fresh and spacious look.

ELEMENTS OF THE STYLE

Harmony is the key to the soft modern style. The newest ranges of wallpapers, paints and furnishing fabrics are comprehensively colour and pattern coordinated for putting together instantly compatible schemes. Plains, stripes, chevrons, trellis, checks and tartans live happily side by side with florals, abstract patterns or imitations of broken colour paint finishes on wallcoverings and fabrics.

Paint effects such as sponging, ragging and dragging are used extensively on walls and woodwork to soften the colours by adding subtle shading and pattern. Limed wood paintwork also adds a distinctive touch of fashionable ageing. Woodwork on doors, architraves, skirtings and window frames is sometimes left natural, and just varnished, as a grainy contrast to plain walls.

In the absence of architectural details, such as cornices, coving and dado and picture rails, you can substitute wallpaper borders to break up the proportions of the room. The dado area is often picked out in a slightly different coloured paint, patterned wallpaper or wood panelling to provide a band of gentle contrast round the room.

Floors are frequently left bare as natural, polished floorboards to serve as a neutral background. Colourful rugs scattered across the floor add comfort and warmth, and provide focal points for grouping furniture. Fibre matting is one step on from stripped and polished boards, yet provides the same hard-wearing, neutral backdrop for the furnishings.

A fireplace with its mantelshelf is a bonus factor in a soft modern living room. The fire surround can be painted to blend in with the walls or picked out in a bolder colour to create a dramatic focal point for the room.

USING FABRICS

The latest fabric designs are used in profusion for upholstery and window dressings. Floor-length curtains add stature and elegance to the room. They can either be left to hang freely to the floor or pulled apart in graceful drapes on each side of the window with stylish tiebacks, tasselled cords or metal holdbacks. In keeping with a desire for simplicity, and the need for privacy and warmth permitting, curtains can be dispensed with completely or dropped in favour of blinds.

ACHIEVING THE LOOK

The understated elegance of this room is typical of the soft modern style. The key design features are pinpointed here to help you assemble a similar look in your own home. Look at the pictures on the following pages to check how these common denominators are used in other rooms, as well as to get more good ideas from alternative interpretations of the look.

WALLS

A softly striped wallpaper supplies the perfect neutral background against which to arrange bolder colours and exciting patterns. A muted broken colour paint effect would create a similar impression.

LIGHTING

Strategically positioned to cast a gentle light round the room in the evening, a stylish limed wood lamp base is in total harmony with the subtle colour scheme.

ACCESSORIES

Novelty bowls, unusual ornaments and a handsome vase of flowers introduce individuality to the scheme. A light wood shelving unit offers vital storage space, while simple line drawings surrounded by solid picture frames perfect the look.

WINDOW

Simplicity is the keynote here – curtains in a large scale floral print hang straight down to the floor from a plain curtain pole.

ACCENTS

The blue check and deep blue covered armchairs strike a distinctive note in this scheme. Strong or contrasting coloured accent features on upholstery and cushions are always a good way of adding extra interest.

SEATING

Sofa and armchairs are soft, comfortable and smartly upholstered. Differing shapes and styles add character to the room.

TABLES

Side tables and coffee tables are very plain in shape, usually made from natural wood on its own, or in combination with metal and glass.

SOFT MODERN FURNISHINGS

Sofas, armchairs and tables with simple, streamlined profiles work best in a softly modern layout. They don't have to be new or high-tech; a comfortable old sofa can be made to look the part with fresh, neatly tailored upholstery. Any harsh angles or sharp edges can easily be softened with a casual throw or stacks of cushions.

Wicker furniture has moved inside from the garden and is now well and truly established in the soft modern living room alongside a conventionally upholstered sofa and armchairs. Padded with comfy cushions, the strong shapes of the cane sofas and armchairs provide smart, easy seating, while their matching tables fit comfortably into the same arrangement.

The mixed and unmatched look of the seating, its upholstery and other soft furnishings in the room is very much part of the soft modern approach. Arranging the furniture in the room to form sociable groupings while leaving plenty of space round each piece is also important.

Metalwork has also infiltrated the soft modern living room in the shape of table and chair frames, candle sconces and curtain rods. Its rugged, minimal good looks suit the pared-down soft modern style.

A low coffee table sited in front of a sofa or between two sofas becomes an indispensable surface upon which to rest drinks, magazines and plants. If there is enough space, a small table positioned in a corner of the room, or behind the sofa, provides support for a tablelamp and vase of flowers or a pot plant.

The sitting room needs generous storage to keep clutter at bay and maintain a stylish, orderly appearance. A well chosen storage and display or shelving system can enhance the restful tidiness of the room.

A few elegant accessories complete the soft modern look and provide an opportunity to stamp your taste on the room. Stylishly simple, clean lined vases and ornaments have the greatest impact, along with one or two groupings of pictures in plain frames on the walls. For a final touch of individuality, you can display items from a favourite collection – even a twisted piece of driftwood from a beachcombing trip adds character to a room.

LIGHTING

By day, the soft modern living room is light and airy. In the evenings, overhead lighting proves too glaring for a relaxed atmosphere. Modern uplighting bracket and bowl wall-mounted fittings diffuse a far gentler background lighting.

Strategically positioned table lamps play an important supporting role. Interesting lamp bases and smart shades provide decorative accent features, while their subdued glow makes the room look warm and welcoming in the evening. Lamps also provide a localized and directable source of light for reading or working.

Candles in shapely candleholders and wall sconces are a popular source of incidental, soft lighting. They cast a kindly flicker of light over the room, mellowing edges and contrasts.

▲ Follow the pattern
It only takes a few flashes of bold coloured pattern to give this all white room its soft modern lift.

◨ Special details
Colourful flowers, cushions and rugs make a simply furnished room look warm and welcoming.

◀ *Neutral hints*
There are times when pastel colours can be treated as token neutrals. Here pale green walls work happily with the floral print upholstery and flourishing pot plants to give the room a fresh, outdoor feel.

◣ *Dressing up*
A large bay window like this can carry off an elaborate curtain treatment without detracting from the easy simplicity of the rest of the room.

DETAILS

Paying special attention to the final details of a soft modern living room makes all the difference to its friendliness and character. With a splash of contrasting colour on a rug or cushion here, an attractive table lamp there, plus the odd ornament, picture and pot plant, you stamp your own personality on the room.

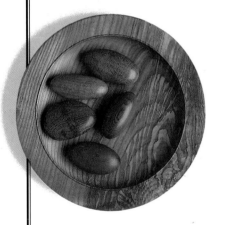

◀ Lighting effects
Stylish table lamps cast more than a gentle light on the soft modern scene. This metal tripod base and neat shade are an eye-catching feature of the room, and perfectly placed to throw light over the shoulder of anyone reading in the armchair.

▼ Thrown in
A colourful rug casually draped over the back of an armchair really brightens up a room. At the same time, it introduces welcome notes of contrast, informality and comfort that suit the soft modern spirit.

◀ Added interest
Displaying unusual ornaments, like this wooden plate with its clutch of wooden eggs, in a room adds a personal touch with an exciting originality.

▶ Floral dash
Growing pots of flowering plants and displaying them in novelty containers creates a movable and changeable feast of colours that will wake up any room.

GLOBAL LIVING ROOMS

*You don't have to be well travelled to appreciate the joyful
colours, chunky furniture and exciting accessories that give the global living
room such a relaxed, contemporary feel.*

As the world seems to shrink, with tourists venturing to far-flung corners of the globe, the vibrant crafts and exotic artifacts of different cultures have rapidly infiltrated the latest trends in home and fabric design. Global style is essentially an unstructured blend of the rustic and the elegant, which is an ideal combination for uncluttered living areas where the emphasis is on relaxation.

The great attraction of the global look lies in its appealing combination of natural materials, simple practicality and bold use of pattern and colour. Added to which, many of the basic elements of the look – rugs, textiles, decorative objects and even furniture – are handmade and display a refreshing originality when compared with most mass-produced goods. Fortunately, you don't have to wander too far to find the ingredients for recreating the look in your own home; many are widely available at economical prices in a variety of outlets from department stores to speciality home shops.

You can create a theme for the look by restricting your choice to elements from one part of the world – the Middle East or India, for example – but the essence of the global village style is an uninhibited combination, where African carvings mingle with Indian prints and Latin American weaves. The result is a peaceful, cheering oasis that soothes the spirit and delights the eye.

*The global style is
an easy-going blend
of pure elegance and
rustic simplicity, in
which rich colours,
elementary patterns
and original
handicrafts play
major roles.*

CREATING THE LOOK

Walls For sympathetic backdrops, choose wall colours from the warm or natural part of the spectrum. Creamy white with dark-stained woodwork recalls tropical climes. You can opt for earthy shades of terracotta, dull red, russet or ochre, washed on in loose, wide brush-strokes for a warmer look. Bare wall plaster, tinted and sealed, makes a suitably luminous surface. As extra definition, you can add a narrow margin of handpainted trim to the top or base of the wall. Repeating simple motifs like diamonds, chevrons, dots or squiggles evokes tribal decoration.

Covering walls with fabric adds an authentic, textural dimension. Nubbly hessian is a good choice. Alternatively, you can staple lengths of printed Indian or African cotton to the wall for a richly layered tented look.

Floors Cool, smooth floors or rugged natural weaves strike the right note underfoot. Stripped wooden floorboards, waxed and sealed or stained a dark mahogany colour make a practical and hardwearing floor. Flagstones and ceramic or terracotta tiles are also eminently suitable, although such hard floors may prove unacceptably chilly in cooler climates.

For wall-to-wall coverage, natural fibre matting is more appropriate than wool carpet. Natural floorcoverings are available in a range of different fibres, including coir, sisal, jute, seagrass and rush. Sisal, in particular, comes in very attractive weaves and subtle vegetable colours. You can lay most natural fibre floorcoverings just like carpet, or you can install a room-sized mat.

All these floorings provide the perfect base for interesting rugs. Flat weaves such as Indian cotton dhurries are economical and easy to maintain; the more expensive kelims are alive with colour and pattern. Felt rugs embroidered with animals, stripy Mexican serapes and rugs bearing intricate geometric designs all provide a decorative feature. Use them singly or overlap them for a cosy, cluttered effect.

Windows The key is simplicity. Formal, tailored or elaborately draped treatments are at odds with the look. Natural cane blinds, plain roller blinds, billowing lengths of white muslin or simple curtains made from hand-woven or blockprinted textiles are far more compatible. Unbleached cotton calico, ikat, batik or kelim designs on bedspreads, or rough textured linens, look good hanging from wooden or wrought iron poles. For a more exotic effect, drape a glittering sari in loose folds over the window and enjoy the jewel-like colours. Wooden Venetian blinds or louvred shutters look right and give more substantial light control.

ELEMENTS OF THE STYLE

The essential simplicity and originality of this living room sum up the characteristics of the global style. The strong use of bold shapes, simple patterns, natural materials and tribal artifacts create the mood. More colourful and exotic interpretations are illustrated on the following pages to help you capture some of the richness and excitement of this look in your own decorating.

SOFT FURNISHINGS
Embroidered with a folk art pattern, scatter cushions supply a vital splash of bright colour. The highly textured throw adds another typically handcrafted touch.

WINDOWS
The window treatment is kept simple, with ample, faintly striped fabric hanging freely from a black metal curtain pole.

LIGHTING
The metal electric candle sconces, hanging on the wall on either side of the fireplace, look suitably primitive. Incidental lighting is provided by plain table lamps positioned strategically round the room. The two metal-fish candlesticks epitomize the look.

WALLS
Bands of abstract pattern, based on a simple repeating chevron motif, are stencilled in warm beige on to plain white walls, providing a colour link with the upholstery fabric and wicker furniture.

FURNITURE
Sensible seating like the chunky sofa is upholstered in a yarn-dyed checked fabric in mellow tones of cream and beige. Twin footstools double as coffee tables, supplemented by little side tables in natural wicker and metal, and a matching magazine rack.

ACCESSORIES
A variety of handcrafted accessories is vital in establishing the look. The terracotta vase, wooden tray, wire fish and framed native American design introduce a sense of different cultures. Even the flower arrangement on the mantelpiece has a luxuriant, tropical feel.

FLOOR
Neutral carpeting sets off the furnishings, while an informal cotton rug absorbs the wear and tear between the seating.

GLOBAL-LOOK FURNISHINGS

Furniture The emphasis is on comfort and informality. The type of furniture which is generally associated with outdoor living, verandahs or conservatories works well in this situation. Generous wicker chairs and sofas with deep, squashy cushions, planter's chairs with slatted reclining backs, upholstered ottomans and big floor cushions invite lounging and relaxation. Cane tables and chairs, rattan pieces with wrought iron legs and basket chairs have the same indoor/outdoor quality. Dark carved chests, African stools, wicker hampers or low cane tables can serve as occasional or coffee tables to anchor the basic seating arrangement.

You can fashion robust upholstery from plain calico, ikat or kelim designs. Layer sofas and chairs with Indian paisley shawls, crunchy cotton throws or lengths of handcrafted embroidery. Indian embroidered textiles inset with twinkling mirrors, Latin American appliqué or sumptuous batik make eye-catching cushion covers. You can afford to be lavish with inexpensive Madras cotton bedspreads.

Lighting Simple glass lanterns, pierced metal hanging fixtures and polished brass lampbases with wide, flat shades blend comfortably with the look. Pendant fittings in bamboo and paper, upturned waxed paper parasols and the standard paper globe suggest an Eastern influence. Fabric-covered shades in ethnic designs make an apt topping for plain ceramic or pottery bases.

Accessories Indian mirror frames meticulously pieced from a mosaic of mirror and coloured glass sparkle on the walls. African or Indian framed prints supply the right atmosphere. Large baskets and hampers are versatile accompaniments. Flourishing ferns or tropical plants housed in brass or basketry containers create jungly settings. Exotic hothouse specimens, such as protea or orchids, enhance the global theme.

The list of appropriate mood-capturing ornaments is endless – carved African animals or heads, Mexican tin ornaments and painted ceramics, soapstone vases, carved boxes inlaid with mother-of-pearl, brass platters and intricate candlesticks or appliquéd hangings and throws merely set you thinking along the right lines.

▼ Worldly goods

Kelim-style cushions and upholstery bring a neutral scheme to life. Originally more at home in Middle Eastern dwellings, the raw earthy colourings of the kelim patterns have adapted well to modern interior designs.

▲ Aladdin's cave

A treasure-trove of exotic fabrics is a good way to set up a global scene. Spicy colours and rich silks and brocades are a dramatic contrast to solid wooden furniture and natural floorcovering.

◄ Cameo role
A small grouping of tribal carvings and an old cooking pot on a rough wooden table looks charming and has great curiosity value as well.

▼ In from the verandah
The basics of the global look are often borrowed and adapted from items that fulfil different roles in warmer climates. Here, sturdy wicker furniture forsakes the garden to slot easily into a global-look living room. Bright rugs, deep-gusseted cushions and colourful scatter cushions add comfort.

The global style affords an opportunity to collect and display treasures from around the world. These simple artifacts, handcrafted from natural materials, display an originality and creativity which is irresistible.

△ Individuality
A simple geometric pattern gives this chunky terracotta bowl a character all its own.

△ The world at your feet
Traditional motifs from Persian rugs are woven into a multicoloured broadloom carpet to provide an exotic background for global-style furnishings.

◁ Global inventions
Ancient tribal motifs are great sources of inspiration for present day designers. The dynamic patterns on these fabrics, wallpapers and borders, for example, are inspired by traditional motifs from a range of cultures; mix and match them to create stimulating interior schemes.

▷ Fishy business
Quirky, handcrafted accessories like this wooden fish are an essential feature of the look and great fun to collect and display.

▽ Tidy minded
A cane and metal magazine rack is a practical accessory with natural appeal.

APARTMENT LIVING ROOMS

*Bright, cheerful and inexpensive to put together, the
modern apartment look is crisp, streamlined and right up to date. Stylish as
well as practical, it makes a room that's fun to live in.*

T he modern apartment look is ideally suited
to a first home where space is likely to be at a
premium and funds are somewhat limited.
To decorate the living room in this look use
light airy colours to create a relaxed, spacious
feel, as well as to provide a neutral background
for brighter fabrics, rugs and upholstery.

For a scheme that's neat and sophisticated yet
easy to live with, it's important to make the most
of the space you have by planning practical storage solutions to avoid clutter, and choosing key

items of furniture on a suitable scale for the
room. If you are buying new furniture, select
classically simple shapes that will look good
anywhere. Look for hardwearing upholstery
fabrics in happy, vibrant colours. Or hunt around
for good secondhand pieces that you can cheer
up with a fresh coat of paint.

Finally, add individual style by displaying a
few of your favourite accessories – eye-catching
modern prints and bold ceramic vases in bright
accent colours fit the bill.

*The modern apartment living
room is bold and stylish.
Simple, streamlined furniture is
upholstered in strong primary
colours. The effect is reinforced
with framed prints, bright
ceramics and glass, and cheerful
scatter cushions.*

SETTING THE SCENE

Walls and ceilings To achieve a feeling of spaciousness, paint walls and ceilings in light colours – dark colours always make a room look smaller than it actually is, and this is the last thing you want when space in your home is restricted.

Avoid highly patterned wallpapers and borders that are too fussy for the look – if you prefer wallpaper to paint, choose one with a subtle pattern or try one of the paint effect papers which look just as good as the real thing. Mottled designs, small geometrics and abstracts provide the right background for the simple styles of furniture.

Make good use of mirrors as they reflect light and give a sense of extra space. There are some lovely styles in different sizes around. Try positioning the mirror to reflect an attractive view. If you are particularly concerned about making the room look bigger and lighter, you could even fit mirror tiles over an entire wall.

Windows Keep window treatments unfussy and window sills free of clutter. Roman, roller or venetian blinds all have the simple linear effect which complements the streamlined furniture. Alternatively, choose tailored curtains with neat pinch or pencil pleat headings. Cotton prints in vivid, primary colours add a lively touch; or, for a more quietly elegant setting, choose colours which are strong yet soft – for example use a crushed raspberry rather than a bright red.

Floors For a clean, fresh look, go for wooden floorboards that are sanded and polished, or woodstrip flooring. Brighten up the bare boards with a plain wool or heavy cotton rug, or one with a bold abstract or ethnic pattern. Natural fibre matting is also suitable; it's inexpensive, hardwearing and looks good with most furnishing fabrics.

For more comfort and warmth underfoot, choose fitted carpet which blends with the walls, ideally in pale or neutral colours. Fitted carpet always makes a room appear bigger than it really is – even more so when you choose a light, airy shade and a simple pattern.

CHARACTERISTICS OF THE LOOK

The clean, spacious feel and bright accent colours are typical of the modern apartment look. The main features are pointed out here to help you recreate the look in your home. Look at the pictures on the following pages for more ideas you can adapt.

WALLS

White walls and ceiling give the room a light and airy feel while providing a plain background for modern prints in vivid colours.

FURNITURE

Seating is low and casual in style, upholstered in sunny, primary colours. Scatter cushions add extra comfort and colour.

STORAGE

Open shelving, wall cupboards and roll fronted low cabinets provide ample storage for a range of different items. Painted in a coordinating cool green, they stand out well against the white walls.

TABLE AND CHAIRS

Create a separate dining area where space permits. Choose simple, unobtrusive designs, leave wood natural or paint it to coordinate with soft furnishings.

ACCESSORIES

Stylish modern ceramics, painted wood and papier mâché are all appropriate for the look. Pot plants provide fresh and inexpensive natural decoration all year round.

LIGHTING

Plug-in standard and table lamps can be moved to where they are needed, while a pendant light on a long cord casts soft but direct light over the whole room.

CREATING THE STYLE

Lighting The numerous different activities for which the living room is used mean that you will probably need to combine several kinds of lighting. Plug-in table and standard floor lamps are a good practical choice as they can be moved to highlight different areas. For a smart look choose sleek, modern designs.

If you prefer overhead lighting, avoid a harsh effect by hanging a pendant lamp on a long cord over a table or recessing downlighters into the ceiling. For effective accent lighting (to highlight pictures, shelves or plants) use adjustable wall or ceiling-mounted spotlights which are available singly or in groups on a track. For extra mood lighting add plain plaster or ceramic bowl wall lights.

Furniture Seating is classically stylish but casual. Upholstered sofas and chairs are often soft and unstructured, generally featuring low backs – tall furniture can make a small room feel cramped. Go for cheerful fabrics in stripes, checks or bold plain colours. Coordinating plain and complementary patterned cushions add comfort and interest.

The focal point of the room is often a low coffee table, perhaps incorporating a magazine shelf, set centrally within easy reach of the armchairs and sofa. Choose tables with simple lines, either white or black lacquered or made of light woods which you can paint, stain or leave natural. A glass topped table is unobtrusive and opens up space in a small room.

Storage Make the most of fitted storage space. If you have a chimney breast, consider putting up shelves in the alcoves on either side; doors can be fixed to the lower shelves, for unobtrusive, concealed storage.

Freestanding, wall-to-wall storage units look smart – self assembly systems which consist of different individual units are the most practical. Usually white or black lacquered, or made of natural pine, units can be adapted to your needs, with open shelving for books and videos, space for lamps and ornaments, drawers for odds and ends or glass-fronted cabinets for china and glass. In a small living room, restrict such storage to one wall if possible, and avoid tall, dark units. Instead opt for glass shelving which has a light, airy feel.

Hinged window seats, old chests and wooden boxes could be used for extra storage as well as providing original side tables or extra seating. Trolleys, usually chrome or black metal, make flexible storage systems for stereo systems, videos and televisions which can then be moved safely and easily if necessary.

◀ *Work, rest and play*
Advantage is taken of the recessed area behind the door to build a home work station, while ample storage ensures that the rest of the room is kept clear.

◀ *School for style*
A disciplined colour scheme sets
the scene for unusually shaped
accessories. Here, storage
cupboards are colourwashed to
coordinate with long cushions
and a kidney-shaped coffee table.

▼ *Primary school*
Modern accessories such as the
chrome wall clock and wrought
iron and glass candlesticks
look appropriate in this
apartment style room, where
the emphasis is on simple
streamlined furniture and
intense colour.

▼ *Natural comforts*
A neutral colour scheme is
particularly suitable for making
a small room feel bigger. Here,
the mobile storage system is
extendible if necessary.

DETAILS

Accessories to complete the look should be carefully selected and displayed – unnecessary clutter will ruin the sleek appearance of the room. Plain walls are the ideal background against which to exhibit colourful prints and posters or dramatic black and white photographs set in inexpensive plain wood, metal or simple glass-and-clip frames.

◀ Budget ideas
For instant colour, fill bright ceramic vases with flowers or choose pot plants with glossy leaves which provide a year long green touch.

▲ Corner filler
A compact, fold-away table is a sensible choice when space is tight. Here the texture of the cane top adds warmth and interest to the scheme.

▼ Bright lights
Novelty shaped candles are an inexpensive way of introducing colourful style to an apartment style living room.

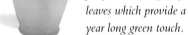

◀ A stack of style
A bold modern colour scheme can take strongly patterned accent features like these striped and checked cushions.

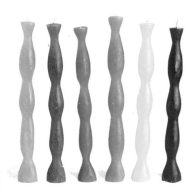

▶ Simple touches
Plain, colourwashed wooden furniture contrasts well with boldly patterned, ethnic-style accessories in lively colours.

SMALL LIVING ROOMS

Big drawing rooms and huge parlours are largely things of the past – in most homes a small living room is the norm – but making the most of a limited living space is mostly a matter of careful planning.

M ost families nowadays are likely to live in a house or flat with one or two fairly small reception rooms. Sometimes the dining room is separate, in other cases it is part of the living room, but rarely is there space to allow for separate living, dining and play or study rooms.

Family living rooms are the most difficult to plan, as they have to meet the needs of different age groups and change with a growing family. This is aggravated if the space is small and the room used for a variety of recreational pursuits – from relaxing in front of the television set to keeping young children entertained or receiving guests.

The first step to overcoming the confines of a small living room is to look closely and in detail at the way the room is used. How many people do you need seats for on a daily basis? Do you do much entertaining and, if so, can you borrow extra chairs from other rooms? What do you really need to store in your living room? Are there any recreational activities that you can move to another part of your home? Can older children play board games in their bedroom, for example?

Once you have the answers to these questions, you can start transforming the space into a well planned, well organized and perfectly functional attractive living area.

The focus is on seating in this small living room. Although filled with large-scale pieces of furniture, it escapes feeling overcrowded by virtue of its pale colour scheme in white and beige. Light colour on the walls and low ceiling makes them recede, while the outline in piping catches the eye and adds definition.

PLANNING

For a small living room to function efficiently you need to plan it down to the minutest detail. Well designed storage, though it eats into the available space, clears the room of clutter, giving it a streamlined appearance. The more storage you build in, the larger the room appears to be.

Don't be afraid to build up if there isn't room to build out. Although high level storage is not usually very accessible, there are always a certain number of items that need to be stored even though they are rarely used.

Most people hoard possessions and this state of affairs is aggravated tenfold in a family living room – children's paraphernalia takes up an enormous amount of space. Banish private possessions to bedrooms and leave living rooms for home entertainment equipment – records, tapes, CDs, videos, books and games.

If you are starting from scratch, built-in seating units – as an alternative to sofas – may help to solve the problems of small living rooms. The advantage of built-in seating units is that they take up considerably less floor space. Units are rarely as deep as sofas and, as they are positioned against the wall, they follow the contours of the room, so making the most of the available space. You can create banquette seating units which have a generous amount of storage under the seats. You can also run low-level radiators under seating units, freeing the wall space a traditional radiator would occupy.

If you have a bay or bow window, an ill-fitting sofa placed in front of it wastes valuable space and looks awkward. On the other hand, a built-in window seat, decked with cushions, is stylish and efficient in its use of space.

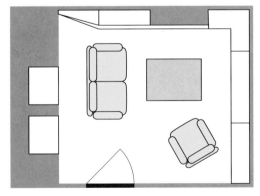

▲ *With one wall of storage to keep the books on display and hide away most other items, this room is easy to keep tidy. Two-seater sofas provide seating, flanking a coffee table. The glass top makes the coffee table a less imposing option than one in, for example, dark wood.*

◄ *Installing built-in cupboards and shelving is a good way to create plenty of storage without intruding into the room. The storage in this attic room makes use of the low ceiling area, which would otherwise be unusable. The furniture is kept to a minimum, so the room isn't overcrowded.*

FURNISHINGS

Keep colour schemes light and unfussy – pale colours, small-scale patterns and matching or coordinating fabrics for upholstered furniture all work well in a small room.

Consider using special paint effects, such as sponging or dragging, to decorate your walls, because applying a glaze over a base colour gives an illusion of extra depth as well as adding interest. This three-dimensional quality can be as subtle as you like. There does not need to be a huge contrast between the colours of the base and the glaze for it to work.

Keep window treatments as simple as possible – complicated or lavish drapes, fussy pelmets and extra-long curtains which puddle on the floor may easily overwhelm a small room.

Furniture should be neat and compact. Low-backed easy chairs create an impression of space. Versatile furniture, such as a blanket box that serves as a coffee table, combines two functions within the one piece – vital if your living room is full to bursting point. A storage unit along one wall, with cupboards below for out-of-sight items and open shelves for TV, stereo, books and ornaments, gives a sense of order while still looking friendly.

▼ *You can have a few large items of furniture in a small living room, as long as you make them the focal point of the room. Here, the three-seater sofa takes pride of place. The rest of the furniture is of a suitably small scale and delicate design for the room size. A triangular cupboard makes good use of the corner of the room, providing storage and displaying ornaments without taking up valuable room space.*

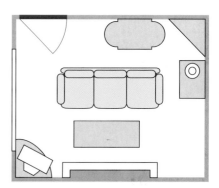

The most traditional way of making a small room appear larger is by means of mirrors. Either hang framed mirrors in strategic places – such as over a fireplace – or opt for a larger expanse of plain sheet mirror. A good way of widening a narrow room is to place long mirrors on either side of a window. Alternatively, emphasize any alcoves by covering their walls with mirror panels.

Good lighting does a lot to maximize a small space. Try to make the lighting fixtures themselves as unobtrusive as possible, with carefully positioned wall or ceiling-mounted lights providing the main output, rather than standard or table lamps. At the same time ensure the scheme delivers a good level of light that reaches right into the corners of the room – halogen spotlights, with their clear, sparkling light are perfect for this. Also, make the most of natural light by placing a mirror opposite a window to reflect daylight into the room.

▶ *Using a window seat in place of the more traditional choice of sofa or armchair is a stylish use of space and natural light, and gives a good view in comfort. Window seats can be just as comfortable as sofas, too – just add lots of cushions. Here, the cushions coordinate with the window blinds.*

◀ *This compact low-level fitted arrangement in two tiers provides both storage and surface space and ensures that most of the walls are kept free for pictures and prints, emphasizing a feeling of space in a small room.*

▲ *Boxing in the low-level radiator under this window lets you use it as a shelf, occasional table or even a seat.*

LIVING ROOM SEATING

As well as looking good in a living room, seating that's well arranged and comfortable will help people relax and encourage the flow of conversation.

The choice of seating, and how it's arranged, makes all the difference to a living room. A seating arrangement that manages to combine comfort with style and is versatile enough to satisfy all that's asked of it is one of the keys to a convivial scheme.

Often the living room has to be all things to everyone – a place for the family to relax together and watch television, read or listen to music; a play space for children; an area for sewing and other hobbies; a room for entertaining, which can lend itself to being dressed up for special occasions. A living room might even sometimes be called on to double as a guest bedroom, if a sofa bed is part of the seating scheme.

Every living room has special requirements, so the first step in planning a flexible seating arrangement is to sit down and see what works well in practice and which elements need to be changed. Would drawing your armchairs and settee closer together lead to a more sociable group? Is the flow of conversation interrupted by people passing through the seating group on their way in and out of the room? Bearing in mind the layout of the room, would a large and a small settee create a more agreeable social group than the traditional settee and two armchairs? Does the TV set dominate the room? Make a note of anything that could be improved, and use the information overleaf to help you organize your priorities.

Two comfortably roomy settees, a two and a three-seater, placed at right angles create a sociable seating group and make good use of limited space. The matching armchair can be drawn up to the group or be pushed back for reading or sewing.

PROBLEM SOLVERS

Look through the list below to pinpoint areas of dissatisfaction in your seating organization. Often the solution is simple – a rearrangement of armchairs and settee into a more sociable grouping can make the room far more workable.

❖ **An awkward room shape?** Rather than shift heavy furniture, draw a room plan on squared paper, marking doors, throughways, windows, fireplace and special features. Measure the furniture and draw it to scale on a piece of cardboard. Cut the shapes out and move them around the plan until you find a good seating layout.

❖ **Need a flexible scheme?** As well as your main seating group, set up a small table or desk and a couple of chairs in a quiet corner for sewing or hobbies – use a drop-leaf table and folding chairs where space is tight. A comfortable small armchair set apart from the main group, perhaps by a window, also adds versatility. Have flexible lighting, too – set a relaxed mood with soft background lighting and use specific task lighting for sewing or reading.

❖ **Does the seating lack focus?** A fireplace is often the focal point – if you haven't one, group the seats around an attractive coffee table, or introduce a focal point such as a display of large plants or fitted wall units on which you can display ornaments.

❖ **Does the TV set dominate the room?** Shift the emphasis by planning your layout so chairs can be turned around or moved, or stand the TV on a wall unit, in a cabinet or on a wheeled base or trolley that can be pulled out for viewing.

❖ **Do children use the room?** When children are around, protect surfaces with covers – throws over sofas and armchairs, a sheet of cheerful PVC over a coffee table – which can be whipped off easily.

▲ *In a small room, corner seating takes up little space. Neat ideas include wall mounted lamps that extend for extra light for reading, and a glass-topped table which appears to take up little floor space.*

▶ *Four facing chairs, all stylishly modern with chambray loose covers, are an alternative to the more usual facing settees.*

▲ *Group a suite around a fire in winter and push seats back to catch the sun in summer.*

▼ *Here, the sofa divides the living from the dining area. A table and rug define the seating group.*

People gathered in a group naturally form themselves into a circle around a focal point like a fireplace. This circle needs to be flexible and self-contained – ideally, it should not be crossed by others. Allow a minimum of 60cm (2ft) for someone to walk past without having to squeeze by people already seated. Leave at least 30cm (1ft) between the edge of seats and a table so people can stand up and sit comfortably.

A three-piece suite, the traditional seating choice, has a three-seater settee and two matching armchairs. To add versatility to the colour scheme, use coordinating rather than matching pieces.

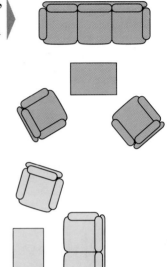

Two roomy, two-seater settees plus an armchair seats the same number as the three-piece suite, and may be more versatile. The settees can face each other across a coffee table, or be placed at right angles. The chair can be moved into or out of the circle.

Flexible alternatives include three chairs and a two-seater settee, or a group of four or five armchairs. For a less crowded look, mix a traditional settee with cane chairs. Draw upright chairs into the seating group when needed.

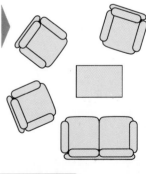

Modular seating made up of armless chairs and corner units can seat more people than conventional suites. Often the corner unit can be replaced by a table. Move extra chairs round to complete the circle when needed.

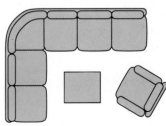

TABLE TALK

An occasional table, perhaps a central one between facing seats, is useful for setting down coffee or drinks, and helps to give a base for the seating. It's also somewhere to display a collection of ornaments or a vase of flowers. Tables don't have to be very large, especially if there is the danger of obstructing a route across the room. A small table at either end of the settee or a square one in the corner of a right-angled arrangement is ideal.

In a long room with a dining area at one end, a narrow table against the back of the settee is an attractive way to define the two areas – it also avoids the problem of having a dead zone behind a settee. Where space is at a premium, consider using a nest of tables, or a glass-topped table which will appear to take up less floor space than a solid one.

◣ *For a first-time buy, keep your options open with a scheme based on one or two well chosen pieces. A settee and armchair and side tables are a practical choice – extra seating can be bought later.*

▶ *When company is expected, an extended social circle can often be created by drawing up extra chairs and borrowing side tables from elsewhere in the house.*

◀ *The two settees in this light, bright living room have a central table and side tables close at hand for both practical and decorative use.*
A lightweight cane chair is a versatile addition as it doesn't take up space or add extra bulk to the scheme and can easily be drawn up when needed.

SOFAS AND SUITES

Buying a sofa or suite is a major investment, so take more than just looks into account. Give size, comfort, construction and the type of cover careful consideration too.

The discomfort of sitting on a worn or badly made sofa or armchair is all too familiar. Like a bed that has seen better days, a sofa with broken springs or seat cushions that have so little padding you feel as if you are sitting directly on the base is uncomfortable and, if you sit in it for any length of time, can lead to troublesome aches and pains.

Comfortable and adequate living room seating is therefore an essential purchase for your home, and, if your sofa is worn or uncomfortable, buying a new sofa or suite should be high on your list of priorities. As with most purchases, cost reflects quality and it is worth allocating as much money as you can afford. Your reward is a sofa or suite that gives you many years of relaxing service.

One of the main considerations is whether you buy a suite, a unit system or sofas and armchairs separately. The advantage of buying a suite – consisting of a sofa and two matching armchairs – is that you can make considerable savings. Furniture retailers are usually able to offer suites at more competitive prices than buying the items individually. However, a suite may not offer the flexibility that you are looking for or suit the room, so it is worth taking the time to plan what arrangement and size of furniture best fits the space before making the final decision.

The key to selecting the right sofa for your home lies in choosing one that's well suited in terms of size and design. This three-seater sofa in a simple cotton check is perfectly in keeping with the style and proportions of this informal living room.

SIZE WISE

Before you even start looking for a sofa, you need to decide on the size. Sofas tend to look smaller in a large showroom, so it is easy to make a mistake and be misled into thinking a large sofa will fit in your living room at home and, just as importantly, through your doorways.

To avoid this, measure up your room and the relevant doorways and draw up a scale plan, including major items of furniture. Use the plan to determine what size and configuration of chairs and sofas best suits the room.

Consider the proportions of the room in relation to the height and depth of the sofa. There is a lot of variation in the height of different sofas according to their style, and if the ceilings are low, a high-backed sofa may dwarf the space just as much as a sofa that is too large.

Also use the simple rule that dark colours advance and pale ones recede – a light sofa makes a room look larger than a darker one. Lastly, always take a tape measure with you when you shop to double check measurements.

▶ *The natural look*
A rattan sofa with loose cotton-covered cushions is the perfect addition to an understated room scheme.

WHAT MAKES A WELL MADE SOFA?

▲ *Sofa cross-section*
A cross-section of an upholstered sofa shows what you don't normally see – exactly what goes on under the cushions and covers. A beechwood frame and springs are covered with a hessian overlay. Layers of upholstery follow – fibre, coir, felt and lastly foam to give the seat a smooth finish – before the damask cover is fitted.

When you look through a brochure or walk through a showroom, you see sofas and armchairs in their finished state, their frames and upholstery hidden beneath attractive fabric covers. What goes on underneath the covers is just as important as their surface appearance, though, so don't be afraid to ask how particular models are made when making your choice. Upholstered furniture is generally made up of four parts: the frame, suspension, filling and covering (sofa covers are dealt with on page 76).

FRAME

Traditional, fully-covered furniture has a strong and springy hardwood frame – often in beechwood – joined by dowels, screws and glue. Modern frames may use staples rather than dowels. Cheaper soft-wood frames do exist, but they have to be more solidly built to take the weight. On sofas and chairs where part or all of the frame is on show – known as show-wood – the frame is usually a hardwood, as softwood dents too easily. Metal and plastic frames are sometimes used, but are not as hardwearing.

SUSPENSION

The suspension is what makes the sofa or armchair comfortable. Traditionally, sofas had large coil springs fastened to a webbing support, but these have largely been replaced by flat zigzag springs, used along with rubber webbing or diaphragms. In some designs rubber webbing completely replaces the springs, while some cheaper types just have blocks of foam laid on a solid chipboard base.

◀ *Mix and match*
You don't have to buy a matching suite. Sofas and chairs in contrasting styles and colours add interest to a room scheme.

FILLING

Top quality furniture uses natural fillings such as horsehair, hessian and wool, but the majority of sofas are filled with foam. New regulations insist that combustion modified high resilience (CMHR) foam is used, so check that this is the case. Make sure that the foam is high density, as low grade foam does not hold its shape as well. Cushions may also be stuffed with feathers. Make sure these cushions are channelled so the feathers do not settle at the bottom. Plumping feather cushions every now and then ensures that they always look their best.

QUALITY CHECKLIST

Regardless of the cost, make sure the furniture is well made. There are certain points to look out for:

❖ If the frame is visible, check for knots, splits and cracks in the wood. Check also that the joints are well made.
❖ Look underneath the sofa or chair for any signs of poor workmanship in the parts that don't show.
❖ Feel the padding. You shouldn't be able to feel the springs through the fabric, or the frame through the seat, back or arms. On foam sofas, look for dome-shaped seats, as foam settles with use.
❖ Pull the arms and back to see how secure they are. They shouldn't have too much give.
❖ Sit down and after you stand up check whether the seat resumes its shape quickly. Sagging seats worsen over time.
❖ Loose cushions should be reversible to even out wear, and loose covers should have generous seam allowances so they won't pull apart in the wash.
❖ Check the finish. Loose threads, poor quality zips and rough edges are signs of poor manufacture.

▲ Leather luxury
Leather has a unique appeal with some practical advantages as well – it shrugs off spills and dust and only looks better with age.

◪ The traditional option
A traditional three-seater and two-seater sofa are paired with a matching armchair with show-wood legs to make up an attractive suite.

COVER CHOICE

A family with children and pets inevitably gives a sofa a harder time than a single person or a couple, so choose the sofa fabric accordingly. Many upholstery fabrics undergo a 'rub' test where they are scoured by a machine until they disintegrate. The higher the number of 'rubs', the more wear-resistant the fabric. Ask a sales assistant about this. Acrylics, heavy cotton, wool, and linen mixed with nylon all wear extremely well. Lighter fabrics such as cotton and chintz aren't so hardwearing and may lose colour and start to look shabby over time.

For heavy wear, it's worth buying a sofa in a patterned fabric which shows dirt and stains less than a plain fabric. Look for a fabric with a stain repellent finish which helps to protect the fabric. Armcaps also protect the most vulnerable part of the sofa or chair from wear and tear. If the service is available, it is worth ordering extra covers for the arms and back to extend the life of the cover. Permanent covers on sofas come in for a lot of wear and tear, so it is often a good idea to choose a sofa with removable covers that you can take off for cleaning.

Bear in mind that fabric on rounded sofas tends to last longer than fabric on boxy designs because it isn't pulled over sharp edges. Baggy covers crease and get dirty more easily than tight ones and therefore wear out more quickly.

New flammability regulations require that sofa covers are flame-retardant, so check that any fabric on your sofa has a flame-retardant backing or is used above a flame-retardant interliner.

When choosing a patterned cover fabric, remember bold patterns can be overpowering in small rooms, while a tiny floral print looks lost on a large sofa or in a big room. For a coordinated style, choose a fabric to match your curtains, but if you have a heavily patterned carpet or curtains, opt for plain upholstery instead, in a toning colour. Many manufacturers offer a basic sofa which they cover for you in your choice of fabric.

If you decide a fabric-covered sofa is not for you, consider leather. It's attractive, hardwearing and needs little upkeep, but on the minus side leather suites are pricey and are cold to sit on.

▲ A modern look

A fixed-seat sofa, upholstered in blue and white is the focal point in this room. Wicker armchairs provide an informal contrast and, toning with the pine coffee table, pull the seating area together.

▼ Straight-armed style

This low-backed three-seater is stylishly simple in design. Sofas with straight rather than scrolled arms often have a more understated feel.

COMFORT AND PRACTICALITY

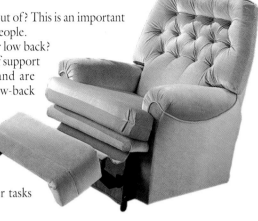

There are many different aspects to consider when choosing a sofa or suite. If you can, take the whole family along to the showroom, so everyone can try out the various designs for comfort. Bear the following pointers in mind.

❖ Only shop when you've plenty of time so you can try out a number of different designs. Never shop when you're tired – anything will feel comfortable.

❖ Take off your coat, sit down and make yourself comfortable. Bounce up and down on the sofa or chair and check that you can't feel the frame or the springs through the cushions.

❖ Make sure your feet touch the floor when you are sitting and the front edge of the seat is comfortable.

❖ Is the seat easy to get out of? This is an important consideration for older people.

❖ Do you want a high or low back? High backs give plenty of support to the head and neck and are better for tall people; low-back sofas may encourage slouching.

❖ Check whether the furniture has castors. These make moving the furniture for vacuuming and other tasks much easier.

◀ *Nostalgic charms*
This roomy show-wood chair in pine has upholstered arms but reversible cushions.

◀ *Choosing the pieces*
If you need less seating than is provided by the traditional three piece suite, why not choose an upholstered stool instead of a second armchair? The sofa and chair have deep seat cushions and scroll arms, while the stool opens up to provide useful storage space.

▲ *Easy living*
Perfect for watching television or relaxing, this armchair reclines, while the front panel extends to provide a comfortable foot rest.

ORDERING YOUR SOFA

Only in very large furniture stores and at sale time is it possible to buy furniture that's ready to go. Most stores don't have the space to keep large upholstered items in stock. Usually the retailer takes your order and passes it to the manufacturer. They then make the furniture, which is delivered 6-12 weeks later.

USING YOUR OWN FABRIC

Most upholstery is offered in a range of fabrics, chosen by the manufacturer as being particularly suitable for that style. The fabrics are also tested for strength, durability and safety, so as well as having a sofa which coordinates with your room scheme, you can be certain it will continue to look good for years to come. However, if you don't like any of the upholstery fabrics on offer, some manufacturers also offer a Customer's Own Material (COM) service, where you can specify a fabric of your own choice. This allows you to combine the shape and style of sofa you like with the fabric you want. Bear in mind, though, that most manufacturers refuse to take responsibility for any wear that may occur with COM.

Fabric options

This two-seater sofa comes in a range of different fabrics. As illustrated here, different fabrics give a sofa a completely different look – the lush floral suggests a cottage style, the red design exhibits a global quality, while the two-colour pattern has an air of pure elegance. To test the appearance of a fabric, whether it is your own choice or one suggested by the manufacturer, it is worth draping a large piece on the chosen sofa and standing back to see the effect before making a final decision.

LIVING ROOM STORAGE

Whether modern or traditionally styled, living room storage gives you a chance to organize all the paraphernalia of day-to-day living in either built-in units or individual freestanding items of furniture.

Choosing storage for a living room is a complex business, since this busy room performs many functions which need to be reflected in both the quantity and type of storage chosen.

This room is the place where you watch TV and listen to music, so you may need to store quantities of video tapes, cassettes and CDs. As well as ornaments, there are books, magazines and papers, and you may also need storage space for china, glass, cutlery and table-linen if the room is used as a dining area.

Almost everyone underestimates how much storage they need. Start by making a list of everything you want to store – both now and in the future. There are some items that you want to display and others you'd rather hide from view, so split your list into the three types of storage – items for display, items to be kept in drawers and those that need cupboard space.

Storage is available in a huge choice of different finishes from the palest pine through to medium shades of oak, mahogany and rich, deep rosewood. Whether in traditional or modern style, much wooden furniture has a veneered surface, bonded to a humbler base such as chipboard that won't warp or twist. Pine, beech and elm are often used as solid woods, or there are coloured finishes in melamine, lacquer or stains.

With so many storage options to choose from, it is worth spending time looking through brochures to be certain of making the right decision for your living room.

Attractive, efficient and plentiful storage is the key to a restful and uncluttered living room. Here, the alcoves on either side of the chimney breast have been put to good use. A mixture of open shelving and cupboard space displays and stores ornaments, books and other belongings.

BUILT-IN OR FREESTANDING?

The type of storage you choose depends on the space you have, the effect you want to create and what you want to store. When it comes to prices, there's little to choose between built-in and freestanding units. Top-of-the-range fitted units are expensive, but you could easily spend the same amount of money on individual freestanding items. Likewise, at the other end of the price range, budget-priced, modular type built-in systems are available and many stores sell budget-priced freestanding ranges.

BUILT-IN STORAGE

Sleek and streamlined, built-in storage is a good idea for small rooms where it can be extended to the full height of the room, if necessary.

Ideal for a conventionally-shaped room, a modular system is based on a series of components, rather like kitchen units, using infill panels where necessary to fill the gaps. It is effectively built-in, though in practice you could take the units apart and move them.

For an awkwardly shaped room, custom-built storage is tailored to fit exactly – utilizing the space in the alcoves on either side of a fireplace, for instance.

FREESTANDING STORAGE

Buying individual items of storage gives you the most flexibility so, if you like to change your room round from time to time, freestanding pieces are the most practical choice. When choosing, price is often a good guide to quality. Self-assembly items are usually cheapest, while top-quality, well-made and finished items in solid pine or veneered woods can last a lifetime.

Choosing freestanding pieces means that as your space alters, or when money allows, you can add items. Always check that the range will be available in years to come.

The only real problem with freestanding furniture is its size. It can be fairly bulky and can make a small room look rather crowded.

▲ Storage wall
Ceiling-height fitted storage covering the entire far wall of this room makes optimum use of space. You can decide just how much space is on show and how much is hidden with doors.

▼ Wall-fixed elegance
This fitted storage in light oak is a mixture of wall-fixed and floorstanding pieces that you put together as you want to make up a complete storage system.

STORAGE CHECKLIST

The kind of storage you eventually choose depends on your lifestyle as much as on your budget and type of home. Refer to the checklist below to make sure you don't forget any essentials at the planning stage:

- ❖ TV and video
- ❖ Videos
- ❖ Stereo system
- ❖ Records, cassettes, CDs
- ❖ Books
- ❖ Newspapers, magazines
- ❖ Stationery, bills and letters
- ❖ Games, playing cards
- ❖ Telephone paraphernalia
- ❖ Drinks, glasses
- ❖ China
- ❖ Sewing, knitting
- ❖ Ornaments
- ❖ Collections
- ❖ Plants

▲ Perfect partners
These two blonde beech wall-hung units complement each other perfectly. The lower one provides cupboard and drawer space, while the other provides well-lit display cubicles – both open and behind glass – for ornaments.

◄ Custom-made choice
Indulging in custom-made fitted living room storage can be a worthwhile expenditure, since it allows you to tailor the storage to your needs and its style to your decor. Here, the shelves are a perfect width and height to display books.

Storage Choice

You can choose from many different types of storage for your living room, or devise your own system from a combination of several types.

Wall-mounted Shelves

An adjustable shelving system is the cheapest way to store a lot of things. Based on a series of uprights which are screwed to the wall, the shelves sit on brackets which slide or clip into the uprights at any height.

If you only have a few things to display, use two or more L-shaped brackets to support a single shelf, or a single long bracket which supports the back of the shelf along its entire length. In alcoves, fit battens to the walls to support shelves.

Veneered chipboard is the most economical choice for such shelves, but only suitable for the lightest items, so if you have heavy things to store, choose solid wood – the thicker it is, the heavier the load it can take. Other shelving materials include plywood, metal and glass. Any glass shelves must be made from toughened glass with bevelled edges for safety.

Open Shelf Units

The cheapest type of freestanding storage, some open shelf units are better suited to heavy storage than others. Available in veneered chipboard, wood, cane and metal, choose units with adjustable shelves for versatility.

Modular Units

The individual sections of a modular unit stack side by side or on top of each other to build into a complete storage system. Highly adaptable, some ranges offer a choice of base and wall units with open shelves, glass or solid-fronted cupboards and drawer units. Others are based on a series of uprights with shelves, drawers and doors which slot or slide into place.

Custom-made Storage

Built-in storage that makes use of an alcove is also an option, but since it involves having the storage custom made from beginning to end, it is fairly expensive. Built-in storage in alcoves on either side of a fireplace can look extremely stylish, however, so you may consider it a worthwhile expense.

Single Units

Some rooms, especially those with period-style furnishings, look best with items of free-standing furniture: a roll-top or knee-hole desk for personal effects; a sideboard for drinks, crockery and glass; and a bookcase or glass-fronted cabinet to house books and treasured objects. A coffee table with a shelf underneath or a magazine rack means that magazines can be kept tidy but also at hand.

◄ **Sitting in the corner**
A traditional pine corner cabinet is the ideal way to bring lost space into play. The light in the glass-fronted cupboard draws the eye to the corner of the room, focusing it on a display of ornaments or flowers.

▲ **Storage in colour**
This modular system has shelving and cupboard space slung between three slim towers, so although robust enough to support a large television, the system has a lighter feel.

DOWN TO DETAILS

❖ **Built-in lighting** is fitted in many wall units. It adds atmosphere and looks especially effective with glass shelves – a great way to show off your favourite glass and china.

❖ **Bar units** have a flap-down door which when open, doubles as a serving area and is ideal for dispensing drinks. You can also use it as an impromptu desk surface.

❖ **Built-in CD and cassette storage** is a useful way to keep track of your music library. Look for trays which pull out for easy access.

❖ **Corner units** are used when storage runs along two walls. Look for wall units with angled fronts for a neat turn.

❖ **Concealed TV, video and stereo systems** improve security and give a more streamlined and sophisticated look to the room. Special units are available to hide them. Sizes vary to suit different sizes of TV set and mini, midi and stacking stereo systems, so always measure up carefully before you buy. TV tables are available where the set is hidden behind a fabric skirt; in other units the TV and video are kept together, with the TV behind doors and the video below in a drawer.

▶ *TV table elegance*

This freestanding cherrywood video unit has an adjustable shelf in the video compartment to store videos of different sizes. The two side drawers are deceptively spacious, storing up to 20 video tapes. The whole unit provides an ideal resting place for the television.

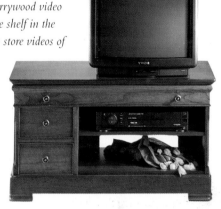

◩ *Complete system*

In warm wood, with display case in contrasting green, this system incorporates room for everything: the modern-day staples of TV and stereo, books, ornaments and even potted plants.

▶ *Freestanding tradition*

The sturdy, rustic appearance of a mellow pine wall unit, with open and glass-fronted shelving, is completely in keeping with this cottage-style room.

❖ Store the things you need most at about waist level with less necessary items above and below.

❖ Shelves for books should be spaced at different intervals to hold various sizes; look for a system with adjustable shelves.

❖ Unless you're very tidy, don't choose only open shelving. Cupboards keep clutter out of sight.

❖ On open shelving, resist the temptation to fill every square centimetre with something – simplicity with just a few items on display is best.

❖ Build a window seat into a bay window and use the space underneath as storage for large items such as toys and games.

❖ Make the most of cupboard space by borrowing a few nifty ideas from the kitchen: a swing out carousel fitted into a corner unit allows easy access to everything stored; wire-tiered shelves screwed to the back of cupboard doors are useful for holding small items; clip-on wire shelves utilize the empty space between the shelves; and a plastic cutlery insert is an excellent way to keep pens and pencils tidy in a drawer.

◪ The DIY option

In an assemble-it-yourself system like this, you select what shelves, drawers and posts you want and build a storage system to suit your needs. Pre-drilled fixing holes along the length of the posts allow you to fix the shelves at any height. Corner units mean that an otherwise neglected area is fully utilized.

◪ Additional space

This set of wooden shelves, with its metal supports placed against a free wall, adds more storage space instantly. Simple in design, these shelves won't overpower a room where the style is already set.

▷ Jigsaw storage

This storage system is fully modular. The shelving to the left is made up of one base unit with two further shelving units stacked on top.

POSITIONING A TV AND STEREO

Choosing where to place your television and hi-fi (stereo) system is as important as selecting the equipment itself – follow a few simple guidelines to make sure you get the best out of these home entertainment purchases.

Nowadays almost every household has a television and sound system, from the smallest CD player with miniature speakers to large-scale televisions with stereophonic sound. Getting the best from your home entertainment equipment depends as much on how you position the units as on the systems themselves.

Once you've decided where to site your hi-fi and television (see overpage) you need to decide how to store and display them. Many living room storage systems offer a module for the television, video and hi-fi, but there are also a huge number of stand-alone units which are specifically designed to house them.

If your home is hi-tech and modern you can make a virtue out of your viewing and listening equipment and choose it to suit the style and decoration of the room. However, for more traditionally furnished homes, the overwhelming modern style of audio-visual systems can spoil the atmosphere, so you may decide to hide the equipment away completely.

Before you buy storage for a hi-fi system, consider how you use the equipment, whether there is adequate access to it – most hi-fi systems require access from the front and top – and where abouts in the room you want to place it. The key to enjoying your hi-fi system at its best is to position the speakers where they give the highest quality sound. This depends to a large extent on the shape of the room and the type and size of speaker – some are designed to sit on the floor, some on a shelf or mounted on a wall and others are designed to be used with a rigid stand.

The most important aspect of television and video recorder storage is to make sure they are sited where you can see the screen easily. When you buy a storage unit for these items, check that it is the right size and height to house them both, and a suitable design for your type of video recorder – front-loading recorders don't need to be moved for normal operation, but top-loading models need a slide-out shelf below the television or a space above.

Siting home entertainment equipment is all about getting the best sound and picture without letting it dominate the decorating scheme. Here a television housed in a pine wardrobe takes pride of place in a living room. Simply shutting the wardrobe doors changes the room's focal point to the seating area and coffee table.

POSITIONING YOUR HI-FI

The operating height of the hi-fi is an important consideration. You should position the system either low enough so that you can kneel in front of it or high enough for you to stand comfortably while loading tapes or CDs.

Some storage units include room for speakers, but while these look neat, they probably don't give you the best sound quality. The most effective position for the speakers is on the floor or high up on a wall in a corner of the room. Here, the sound output is reflected by the corner walls and the floor or ceiling. If this is not possible, the next effective option is to position them on the floor or near the ceiling against one wall. The further the speaker is from the corner, the more the sound is reduced.

In a small room, the speakers are often so close to the seating area that it is impossible to have any background music without it interfering with the conversation. In such a case, placing the speakers off the floor – either wall-mounted or on a shelf – can help. Wherever you decide to place your speakers, it's a good idea to take time to experiment with a few arrangements to find out by trial and error which one suits you best.

Some of the more expensive speakers are supplied with detailed instructions as to where they should be placed. As these are the result of exhaustive listening tests by designers, it's a good idea to follow them to the letter.

Carpets, curtains, even items of furniture can all affect the quality of sound from the speakers. Bare walls and floors reflect the sound, making it much clearer and bigger, while thick carpets and curtains have a muffling effect.

▲ *This is the perfect bedroom for music lovers. A clever shelf arrangement by the head of the bed doubles as bedside tables and stands for the two speakers. The wall-fixed shelves over the bed make space for the hi-fi, so you can put on music without getting up. A stylish television on a wheeled stand at the foot of the bed is the height of luxury.*

▽ *The sound system and television play the most important role in this room, so they are very much features of the decor. The speaker cabinets – which match the rest of the storage – and the television are all on castors, so you can move them to get the best sound and an uninterrupted view from any seat in the room.*

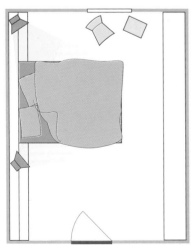

◀ *Speakers on the floor are angled upwards to direct the sound into the middle of the room. An attractive freestanding shelving unit provides room for both the hi-fi and a collection of records and CDs.*

▽ *Shelves cover the whole of one wall in this living room, making room for both the hi-fi and speakers positioned along their length. Putting the speakers at opposite ends ensures that the sound reaches all parts of the room.*

SITING THE SPEAKERS

Each speaker has a cone of sound – the area near the speaker where the sound quality is best. By drawing a plan of your room complete with the main items of furniture, and marking on the speakers and their respective cones of sound, you can work out where you should ideally place them.

▶ *In general,* if you draw a line through the centre of the cone of sound coming from each speaker, the point where the two lines cross is the optimum position to sit and listen to music played on the system. For really serious listening, the distance between the two speakers must equal the distance between each speaker and the listener, forming a triangle of equal sides.

▶ *In a long room,* it is more difficult to position speakers successfully, but it does present more options. If you want a quiet area in the room, for dining perhaps, place one or both speakers part-way down the wall, facing into the listening area; the space behind the speakers is quieter.

▶ *In a square room,* speakers facing diagonally in from the corners of one wall give the whole room sound.

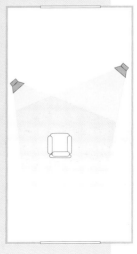

POSITIONING THE TELEVISION

Your television should be easy to view from the most comfortable seats in the living room, but it shouldn't dominate the room. You can meet both of these conditions by placing it on a trolley or keeping it in a cabinet or cupboard with closing doors. However you house it, do make sure that it is on a stand of some sort or placed on a surface to keep it off the floor. The recommended minimum height from the base of the set to the floor is 120cm (48in). This allows you to maintain a good seating posture while viewing. Unfortunately, most commercial stands are much lower than this, forcing you to crane your neck forward or slump in your seat in order to see the screen.

Make sure the television is positioned so that there is minimum reflection off the screen from both the window and any lighting. At the same time, though, it is a good idea to have some lighting near the television when viewing, as looking away from the screen from time to time helps to reduce the eye fatigue caused by focusing on it for a long time. This relief is most effective if you look at something of a similar brightness to save your eyes from having to readjust to different levels of light.

▲ *Unobtrusively placed on a shelf, this television is in a perfect position and at the perfect height to be viewed from the sofa, but surrounded as it is with a collection of pots and books and with a large print on the wall above, it doesn't dominate the area.*

▲ *The space between these built-in cupboards and the shelving above is just the right size for the television and hi-fi with its speakers. All the equipment stands in one spot, so it doesn't interfere with the rest of the room's decorating scheme. Simply turn the television towards you when you want to watch it.*

▶ *This television is cleverly hidden away in a built-in storage system. When you want to watch it, you simply open the door and angle the pull-out stand so it is in the best position for viewing.*

LIGHTING THE LIVING ROOM

Flexibility is the key to creating a practical and pleasing lighting design for your living room – careful planning is the way to achieve it.

From quiet reading to entertaining guests, watching television to tackling homework, the living room caters for a host of activities, many of which take place in the evening. To create a relaxing atmosphere and enjoy your leisure activities to the full, you should pay special attention to the lighting of your living room.

Good living room lighting is all about flexibility. A single overhead fixture won't do the job – even the most luxuriously decorated room appears bland and incomplete when lit by a solitary bulb. The best schemes combine soft background illumination with bright, focused light for reading, sewing or study, and to highlight pictures, treasures or fine features of the room.

When you treat lighting as a key element in the decoration of your living room, you can create subtle areas of light and shade to complement your decor. The wide range of modern light fittings and fixtures available today makes it possible to accommodate all these diverse requirements.

Carefully thought out living room lighting does more than just illuminate the room. The shades and bases of table and standard lamps are attractive features in their own right.

THE BACKDROP

Background lighting takes over from daylight in the evening and forms the foundation for the lighting scheme in a room. Such all-round lighting is generally supplied by permanent ceiling or wall mounted fixtures that are switched on at the door. The overall level of background light can be controlled by installing a dimmer switch.

A ceiling light, whether it is a pendant, recessed or ceiling mounted, is the typical way of providing general lighting. While central pendant lights are the most familiar, with low ceilings, downlighters or ceiling mounted lights are a better option. The light from downlighters is directional so you may need several to provide an all-over background effect. Wall mounted fixtures make good background lighting with their subtle, diffused glow.

A more flexible option is to achieve background lighting with a selection of table and floor lamps, as well as uplighters – as they can be easily moved around to suit changing needs. When the beam from these lights is angled to bounce off a ceiling or wall, it creates an indirect background lighting effect.

▶ *A classic wall uplighter adds atmosphere to the room even during the day. At night it will cast a soft glow over the wall.*

▲ *This small adjustable table lamp is an excellent example of task lighting. Situated conveniently beside the sofa, it supplies a directable beam of light for anyone wishing to sit and read, knit or sew.*

◀ *Concealed local lighting focuses attention on a display of ceramics in the alcove. The good light also shows up the details of colour and pattern in the china very clearly.*

LOCAL LIGHTS

On its own background lighting can be harsh, but teamed with local and task lighting it forms part of an adaptable system. In particular, local light is a vital supplement to the general lighting in a room, setting the mood, defining different areas within the living room and facilitating various activities. A combination of lamps, side lights, uplighters and accent spots in a scheme creates overlapping pools of light, making a room seem much more spacious.

The direction of the light is also important. You need some fittings that give out an all-round glow, as well as more directional fittings to highlight focal points. Table lamps, for example, throw out a cosy circle of light that draws seating areas together and leads the eye from point to point across the room. They also offer the greatest decorative possibilities for introducing extra colour and pattern to a scheme. A plain ceramic or wooden base with a bright shade introduces an accent colour; wrought iron bases add drama; decorated bases insert fresh pattern.

Pinpoint fine features with spotlights, which angle strong beams of light up, down or across an area. Spotlighting is particularly effective when the source is concealed. Hidden behind a wooden display cabinet or bookshelf, small strip lights can be very discreet as well.

Spotlights offer plenty of scope for experimenting with different effects. An object lit from above has a dramatic presence; light coming from below creates a striking silhouette. Glassware makes an exciting, theatrical display when lit from below or behind, especially if arranged on glass shelves. Light pictures from above with an eyeball or ceiling spot to illuminate the picture area.

◻ Here, an angled chrome floorstanding lamp introduces a pleasant modern note among traditional furniture.

◻ During the day this sofa is well lit by the window behind; in the evening, two little table lamps bathe it in a soft glow.

TASK LIGHTING

Having set up the atmospheric lighting in a living room, think about the various activities that take place there and plan extra lighting to suit these specific needs.

For comfort while reading, light should fall on the page from above and behind you. A table lamp positioned to one side or a standard floor lamp placed behind your chair are the best solutions. For work which requires more intense concentration, you may need the boost provided by a desk light. It's hard to better the classic angled desk lamp for task lighting efficiency. This now has extra design potential, since it comes in a range of colours as well as the original black or white.

A single bright light in an otherwise darkened room is very bad for the eyes – which is why it's important not to watch television in the dark. Always ensure that the general lighting provides enough brightness to view the screen without causing eye strain. One solution is to position a lamp behind the set. Another watchpoint is to avoid positioning other lights so that they reflect off the screen.

PRACTICAL MATTERS

If you have the chance, plan your lighting before you decorate. It's best to install a lighting track, recessed downlights and/or fit new power points before you apply final finishes. You may also wish to have floor and table lamps wired to a single switch by the door for extra convenience.

❖ **Make a plan** Measure the living room and draw up a scale plan, marking on permanent features, such as windows, fireplaces and built-in shelving. Mark on the position of existing power points. Then sketch your proposed furniture layout, including the likely position of the television and hi-fi systems. Use your plan to assess whether there are enough sockets to serve your lighting needs, and where built-in light fixtures should be positioned.

❖ **Cost** Low-voltage systems that require individual transformers, and original designer fittings generally cost more. Classic styles in neutral colours outlast any changes of decor and make good economic sense. Any lighting system that requires extensive rewiring adds the extra expense of professional help, together with the cost of redecorating surfaces after the work is completed.

❖ **Dimmers** Fitting a dimmer switch is relatively easy and dramatically extends the range of lighting effects you can achieve. Dimmer switches have a wattage rating, and the fittings controlled by the switch must not exceed this.

❖ **Safety** If you're in doubt about any procedure, call in a qualified electrician; rewiring is professional work. Make sure all plugs are wired safely. Don't overload power points and avoid trailing flexes.

▶ *The look of a room can be altered simply by using different coloured light bulbs. Changing the pink bulb (above right) to yellow (right) and swapping a few accessories, totally revamps the room – but with an image that can be revised at any time.*

◀ *Your lighting scheme is an opportunity to add beauty to your home. An attractive lamp is as important as the welcoming light it provides.*

CANDLE SCONCES

*Whether or not you actually light the candles, pretty
wall-hung sconces can add authentic period detail or a
charming contemporary touch to your decor.*

A lthough gas lighting replaced candles in Victorian times, and was itself eclipsed soon afterwards by electricity, the imagery of candles in wall sconces is reassuringly warm and friendly. The use of candle sconces goes back to medieval times and even earlier, when soft wax or tallow candles were placed on wall spikes in the homes of the wealthy – ordinary people used rush lights dipped in mutton fat or oil. In the 17th and 18th centuries candle sconces became more decorative, made of brass, silver, wrought iron or carved and gilded wood. Some

had glass cups or horn panels to protect the flame from draughts. Today sconces come in a large range of styles and prices, from ethnic and low-cost reproductions to genuine antiques.

Pairs of candle sconces can be hung either side of a mirror, painting or piece of furniture, or either side of an architectural feature such as a door, arch or window. For a luxurious look, add a matching ceiling-hung candelabra. Alternatively, candle sconces can add a nostalgic finishing touch to a bedroom or bathroom; or a warm welcoming glow to a porch.

These elegant Georgian-style sconces, based on a leaf motif, have a suitably prime position above a side table; their gilt finish enhances the shimmering, light-reflective quality of the gilt goblets, table tracery and gilt-framed cameo collection.

▼ *Inexpensive punched tin* candle sconces often have pleasantly informal, early American overtones. As with brass and silver, tin is decorative but also reflects and increases the amount of candle light.

▲ *Traditional gilt scones* enhance the large modern painting in the same way that a gilt frame would, while reflecting the symmetry and period style of the nearby furniture and architrave detail.

▼ *Sparkling showers* of cut crystal or glass add greatly to the beauty and formality of a candle sconce but have a practical purpose as well – increasing, by reflections, the amount of candle light given off.

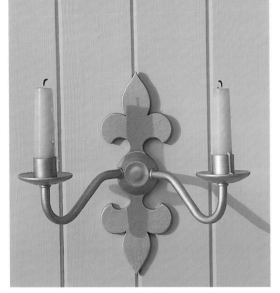

▲ *Combining traditional and modern*, this dulled gilt candle sconce, with its double fleur de lys design, sports bold blue candles and visually holds its own against its sharp, acid-green backdrop.

▷ *Beeswax candles*, with their intricate texture and slightly uneven silhouettes, can look just as charming in a contemporary sconce as in a wrought iron, cottage-style one.

Displaying pictures

Follow some easy shortcuts to success to help you display your pictures to good effect.

It's well worth spending a little time and effort over arranging your picture display: get the positioning right and you increase your enjoyment of the pictures as well as improving the look of the room. Your choice of pictures and how you display them give your room its special individuality, so be guided by personal preference. A few simple guidelines make the task easier and help you avoid pitfalls – pictures hung too high or dotted randomly around the room are two common mistakes. You may want to give favourite or valuable pictures pride of place in your room scheme, while cheerful prints can be used as decorative accessories. You can even use a group of pictures to change the look of a room's proportions – a vertical arrangement makes walls seem higher; with a horizontal display they appear longer.

Enlist some aid when you're arranging a display: have a friend hold a picture in place while you stand back and view it from different parts of the room. Once you've settled on an arrangement, don't feel you have to live with it forever – experiment with different effects by moving pictures around and changing your display every now and then, so that you see your pictures afresh and enjoy them in new situations and from different angles.

Positioning your display

Large, bold pictures usually look best displayed singly, or in pairs, while small pictures are often better carefully arranged in groups rather than just dotted around – see overleaf for possible group displays. Take care when positioning pictures opposite windows because the reflection may make it difficult to see the image clearly. Non-reflective glass may help.

Your pictures and your room scheme will be enhanced if you relate your display to furniture or other features, such as a narrow stretch of wall between two windows. Use main pieces of furniture, or the layout of the room, as a guide to hanging a single picture or a group.

It's also often possible to relate the pictures within a group in some way, whether by subject matter, main colour or a similar colour or type of frame. Perhaps your display could be a mixture of paintings and other collectables. It's fun to have the subject matter of your group of pictures bearing some relationship to the room in which they are displayed – for example, herbal prints in the kitchen, or family portraits in the living room.

Centred display
For a formal arrangement, centre a big, impressive picture or a group of smaller pictures just above a sofa (but not so low that it gets in the way), or over a sideboard or fireplace.

Related to layout
Make use of the room layout, or architectural features – perhaps arrange a small group of prints on a narrow wall between two windows or on a pillar, or hang a big picture above a stairwell.

Offset arrangement
Hang your display to one side of a main piece of furniture for a more casual look, but don't extend the arrangement beyond the width of the furniture or you will spoil the visual effect.

TIP
DISPLAY HEIGHT
The most pleasing height for a single picture or a group display is with the centre of the arrangement at eye level. In a room where you sit and stand – such as a living room – work out the central positions from a standing and a seated position, and site the centre of the display halfway between the two.

A mixed display
For an eye-catching focal point link your display with other collectables – a few pieces of pottery with a picture just above or behind, for example.

Grouping pictures

To display smaller pictures to good effect, gather them into a group. Use the illustrations to help you visualize your pictures within a shape – perhaps a simple row or rectangular block of pictures, or a display set within an oval or even a triangular shape. Align the frame edges to define the boundaries of the group, and take care over spacing, to avoid big gaps that spoil the cohesion of the arrangement. As a rough guide, make sure that the spaces between pictures do not exceed half the width of the smallest picture in the group.

Planning the group

1 Lay your pictures on the floor and shuffle them around until you have a selection and arrangement that pleases you.
2 Measure the distances between each picture and draw a diagram showing their relative positions.
3 Hold the first picture in place against the wall (this could be the centre picture) and make a small pencil mark at the centre top of the frame.
4 Turn the picture over and stretch the picture wire to where it would be if the picture was hanging. Measure from the highest point of the wire to the top of the frame. Measure down the same distance from the mark on the wall to find the position for your hook.
5 Following your diagram, hang the other pictures in the same way.

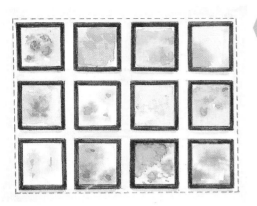

In a block Similarly shaped and sized pictures often look most effective in a simple block arrangement. Take care over spacing, and keep the gaps between the pictures even.

Within a framework Set your pictures within a well defined shape – a rectangle or oval, for example – in an imaginary framework. Balance the display by placing the largest pictures in the corners or the middle of the arrangement. You can emphasize the shape of the display group by framing them on the wall, setting them within a mock wall panel made from ornamental moulding, or use braid, a wallpaper border or a stencilled design as a 'frame'.

Lining up a single row For a horizontal row, range the top or bottom edge of your frames along an imaginary line. For horizontal, vertical or slanted rows (such as up a stairwell) display them with the centres on an imaginary straight line.

Lining up a double row Two rows of pictures can either be lined up centrally, by running an imaginary line between the rows, or be aligned at the top and bottom of the double row. Line up the sides of the outer pictures, too.

In a cross Group pictures round an imaginary cross, with the largest near the centre of the cross balanced by smaller pictures at the outer edges.

BOX FRAMES

Display collector's items and treasured mementoes in a specially designed box frame. It is easy to convert an ordinary picture frame into a box frame, decorated to complement your favourite treasures.

D isplaying small, three-dimensional, collectable objects in an attractive, unified way is always a challenge. By mounting them under glass in a custom-made box frame you can arrange them into a styled mini landscape; and as an extra bonus, the glass and frame will protect the collection from dirt and dust, and give the display an air of permanence.

To make a box frame from an ordinary picture frame, select a frame with a wide surround as this helps to hide the sides of the box, in a shape and size that shows your display to advantage. You can make the box part in two ways. You can either build the sides with wood strips, adding a separate backing board, or you can shape a sheet of expanded polystyrene foam board into a one-piece box. The box

made from wood is sturdier than the one made from foam board, but the foam box is easier to make.

If you don't have a collection of small treasures to frame, it's easy to create one. Choose a basic theme that tells a story and find a frame in a style and colour to complement your selected finds. Themes might be a special occasion, a holiday or a fondly remembered day out in the country, by the sea or visiting a historical site – you'll enjoy collecting all the bits and pieces that build up your story. Memorabilia, like postcards, tickets and photos, make good background collage material, as do pressed leaves or flowers. Alternatively, you can use wallpaper or fabric to set the scene. Once you have chosen the objects for your collection, you can decide how deep to make the box frame.

An elegant glass scent bottle, two dried roses, some pretty lace and an exquisite floral brooch create a nostalgic box-framed display round an old family photograph.

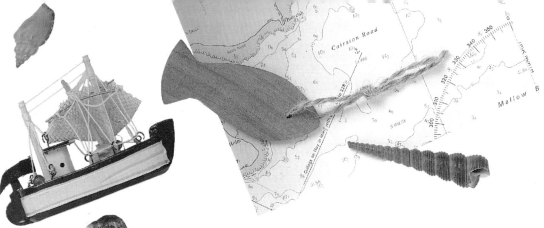

MAKING A WOODEN BOX FRAME

With this style of box frame, the display is fixed to a removable lining panel made from artist's mounting board. The wooden sides of the box are also lined with artist's mounting board. Pick board in a colour to complement the display or cover it with a collage or fabric. If you decide to cover the lining boards with fabric, do this before fixing them in place, for the neatest finish.

The original picture backing board sold with the frame is re-used to secure the back lining panel inside the box frame, and is easily taken off if you want to change the display. When estimating the amount of wood strip needed to make the sides of the box, allow twice the length plus twice the width of the frame. For a box with deeper sides than the one suggested here, use wider wood strip and cut the lining strips to match.

▶ *Satisfy a passion for fishing and all things nautical with a box-framed display of sea fishing mementoes. This collection teams the genuine articles, in the form of a nautical map, fishing net, cork floats and seashells, with a few fun additions – wooden fish and a little plastic tug.*

YOU WILL NEED

❖ PICTURE FRAME

❖ DISPLAY MATERIALS

❖ 12 x 45mm (½ x 1¾in) WOOD STRIP

❖ WOOD ADHESIVE

❖ CLEAR CRAFT ADHESIVE

❖ MOUNTING BOARD

❖ FABRIC OR ALTERNATIVE MATERIALS to decorate lining (optional)

❖ DOUBLE-SIDED STICKY PADS (optional)

❖ PANEL PINS

❖ TENON SAW

❖ CRAFT KNIFE, METAL RULER AND PENCIL

❖ EYELETS AND CORD for hanging the picture

1 Making the wood strip sides Remove the backing board and glass from the frame and set these aside. Measure and cut two pieces of wood strip to fit two opposite sides of the opening at the back of the frame. Use wood adhesive to stick them in place, in line with the edge of the glass rebate. Measure and cut two more pieces of wood strip to fit the remaining sides, overlapping the ends of the pieces you glued before. Stick these in place and leave the glue to dry.

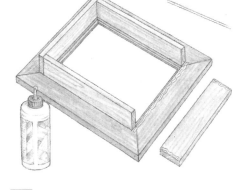

2 Cutting the side lining panels Replace the glass in the frame. Measure and mark two 4cm (1½in) wide strips of mounting board to fit inside two opposite sides of the box, and cut them out using a craft knife and metal ruler. Cut two more strips to fit the remaining two sides. Cover the linings with fabric if you wish (see left). Stick the linings in place with clear adhesive and decorate them as required.

LINING THE BOX WITH FABRIC

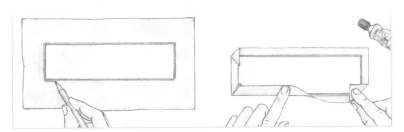

Measure and cut the lining panels as described in step 2 above. Trim off a sliver of board from one short edge on each panel to allow for fabric bulk. Lay the fabric flat, wrong side up, and put the panels on top. Draw round the panels, remove them and cut out the fabric 1cm (⅜in) outside the lines. Lay the panels back centrally on the fabric. Spread a little clear adhesive round the edges of the boards, and press the fabric overlaps on to this, neatly mitring and sticking the corners.

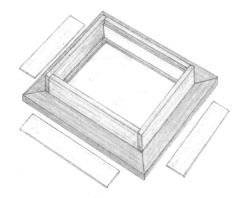

Making the back panel Cut a piece of mounting board the same size as the picture frame's backing board. Decorate this panel to match the box sides, ready for you to arrange the display on it.

Arranging the display Starting with the flattest background material, then building up the display, stick the items in place, using double-sided sticky pads or adhesive as appropriate. Check that the display is no deeper than the box sides. Leave it flat until any adhesive has dried.

Assembling the box Carefully place the mounted display face down into the back of the frame, so it rests on the lining panels. Place the backing board on top and secure it with panel pins. Fit eyelets and cord as required for hanging the picture.

MAKING A FOAM-BOARD BOX FRAME

This style of box frame is most suitable for small frames and those with lightweight displays. As the display material is fitted inside the pre-shaped box, you can drape or extend design elements across the backing and over the inner sides of the box, to create a sweeping, panoramic effect.

Foam core board, which comprises a sheet of expanded polystyrene foam covered on both sides with paper, is available from artists' suppliers, in various thicknesses. Choose the weight most suited to your display.

Cover the inside of the box with coloured paper, fabric or a collage to create an attractive background. Spray adhesive is best for sticking the background in place. As it creates a fine, sticky mist, protect surrounding areas with plenty of newspaper before you use it.

1 Marking the box shape Remove the glass and backing from the picture frame. Lay the glass centrally on the foam board and draw round it lightly. Remove the glass from the board.
For the box base Mark a second line the thickness of the foam board inside the drawn outline. Erase the original outline.
For the box sides Measure the depth of your largest display object and add 1mm (¹⁄₁₆in). Extend the sides of the box base by this measurement. Draw a line all round, connecting the extended lines.

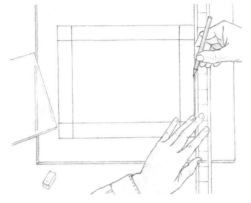

2 Shaping the corners Use a craft knife and ruler to cut out the box around the outer edge. At one corner, mark a line the thickness of the foam out from one inner marked edge (**A**). Repeat to mark the facing inner edge of the opposite corner. Mark the other two corners in same way. Cut out the corners along the new lines. Score lightly through the paper surface along the base edges and ease the box to shape. Mark the two slightly taller sides level and trim to match.

3 Lining the box Flatten the box sides and spray the surface with adhesive. Smooth coloured paper (or fabric or collage) over the adhesive. Trim the paper in line with the box edges. Fold up the box sides and secure them with masking tape.

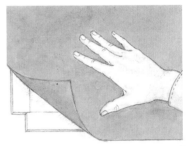

◀ *Exquisite golden embroidery and a dried rose form the romantic contents of this box frame. Gold lettering painted directly on to the glass enhances the three-dimensional effect.*

4 Arranging the objects Stick the objects in place, starting with any flat, background elements. You can also stitch objects in place as a needle and knotted thread pushes easily through the foam board. Leave the box flat on its back until any glue has dried.

5 Assembling the box frame Spread adhesive along the top edges of the box. Supporting the glass with your hands, place the frame over the box. Leave until the adhesive is dry. Secure the joins with strips of masking tape.

LIVING ROOM RUGS

For adding subtle textural contrasts or bold blocks of colour to a room, think of your floor as a horizontal canvas and a rug as the paint.

A single rug can often make the difference between visually dead and visually vibrant decor. Unlike a fitted carpet, which is a major long-term investment, rugs can be bought with a more adventurous approach and moved from place to place as the spirit takes you. While some are costly, many are modestly priced.

Choices range from rustic braided, hooked and rag rugs to Middle Eastern kelim, bokhara and Turkish rugs, Indian dhurries, Chinese and Persian rugs and shaggy Greek flotakis. Materials range from coir and rush to cotton, wool, silk and manmade fibres.

Rugs can enhance a bare or carpeted floor, especially a neutral-toned one. Smaller rugs can read as islands surrounded by a sea of floorboard, tiles or carpet; very large rugs can appear as fitted carpets, with a sliver of underlying floor visible round the edge. Rugs can help define a sub-area of a room – a living room suite, for example, is visually unified and strengthened if the various pieces of furniture are grouped round a central rug.

As well as visuals, consider where rugs can add comfort – on bare floorboards, for example. For safety and to prevent rugs walking, especially at level changes, use mesh backing or nylon bonding strips.

In heavy wear areas, choose colours and patterns that don't show dirt and a texture that takes kindly to vacuuming.

A visual keystone for a suite of wicker furniture, this kelim-style rug, with its natural colours, repeats the colours of the scatter cushions and enlivens the cool green, all-foliage house plant display.

◪ *White on white* can be an exercise in textural contrast and add sophisticated designer overtones to even the most modest scheme. This inexpensive white cotton dhurri throw rug adds a touch of class to a white-painted floor and walls, white sofa and creamy beige armchair.

◪ *A simple circular rug* acts as the bull's eye focal point in this modern living room. The rug reflects the decor's emphasis on natural materials, especially wood; its shape echoes the geometric theme of circles and straight lines; and its cream and blue-grey tones continue the restrained colour scheme.

◪ *The red border* of this living room rug complements the carpet and tartan throw, and picks out the red pattern on the sofa upholstery. Combined with an open fire and wood panelling, the overall effect is of warmth and comfort.

▸ *A tufted rag rug* is ideal for brightening up a fireside, children's room or front door. Small rugs can also be hung on walls as alternative works of art.

CLEVER COFFEE TABLES

*Your coffee table occupies centre stage in your living room –
with a bit of imagination you can make it a real show piece, and a
topic of morning coffee conversation in its own right.*

When you have lavished attention on decorating and furnishing your living room, why settle for just any old coffee table? It can be as unusual and unexpected as you want it to be. Chests, baskets and blanket boxes can all become coffee tables with a difference. The only requirement is that they have a flat, level top to support plants, flowers, books, magazines – and trays of tea or coffee, of course.

A sheet of strengthened glass makes an ideal top. You can see the base and the table seems to take up less space – an advantage in a small room. You can enhance the tabletop by trapping pictures, pressed flowers or pretty fabric between two sheets of glass. A glass merchant will supply sheets of suitable glass cut to size.

The base needn't be a single solid piece. Large jars, vases, pots, urns and carved stone or moulded concrete garden ornaments can all make attractive end or corner supports for a glass top, provided they are level. And if you don't like glass you can always make a top out of a sturdy piece of wood or board, and decorate it in whichever way takes your fancy.

Inspired by stacked storage pallets, this coffee table incorporates four boards that can be pulled out separately when required to extend its useable area.

◄ A pair of baskets placed side by side makes an impromptu coffee table. Baskets like this, or a chest or blanket box, all make practical tables that include additional storage.

► Two beautiful planters support a wooden board, rounded and painted to match, to form a stylish and practical coffee table.

◄ An inexpensive table made from a painted and rope-handled pine packing crate conjures up all the flavours of the East – not the least of them delicious fresh coffee.

► Strengthened glass has been laid over a terracotta strawberry pot, complete with plants, to make an unusual coffee table.

◄ A mobile coffee table goes wherever you want it to. Here four wheels have been fixed to a painted board to create a smart and simple piece of modern furniture.

WAYS WITH TABLES

Dressing up small tables with fancy cloths and colourful rugs acts like a breath of fresh air in a room by introducing new colours, patterns and styles to revitalize the whole setting.

Whenever you want to give a room an instant facelift, one immediate answer is to cover up a little corner or bedside table quickly and inexpensively with an eyecatching cloth or a clever wrap-round drape. At a more practical level, such a cover will also protect a fragile or valuable table and disguise a damaged one.

Pretty, ready-made tablecloths make fine covers, but it's more effective – and more amusing – to improvise your own from shawls, kelims or rugs, or make one from a favourite fabric, trimming it with braid, fringing or colourful ribbon.

Simplest of all, just throw the fabric over the table and leave it hanging loosely. For a more stylish effect, drape the fabric round a plain table in elegant swags and fix it in place with a few strategically positioned stitches or a length of cord, ribbon or tape.

One of the quickest ways to give a small pedestal table a smart new look is to wrap it in a large piece of fabric, held in place with a length of tasselled cord.

◪ **For an Indian flavour,** buy a self-assembly round table, cover it with a red circular floor-length cloth, topped with a large brass tray – or sheet of brass, cut to fit – then trim it all round the edge with a length of gold fringing. Garnish it with Indian ornaments to complete the exotic disguise.

◪ **The exquisite embroidery** and deep fringing on a beautiful shawl can be admired every day when it's used as a full-length cloth over this little bedside table. It is also happily colour coordinated to the pattern on the wallpaper and soft furnishing fabric.

◪ **An old kitchen table** was saved from the scrap heap for its important new role in this corner showpiece, where it's shrouded in colourful rugs. While the rich colours and patterns on the rug and kelim attract all the attention, the table hides modestly – and unsuspectedly – away underneath.

FLORAL CUSHIONS

Whether modern or traditional, complementing nearby curtain or upholstery fabric or introducing a new colour or patterned theme, plump floral cushions are comfortable and pleasing to the eye.

Floral-patterned scatter cushions on a sofa have their own unique charm. The more you have, the merrier – and the more comfortable they are to sink into. In design terms, grouped floral cushions can emphasize the floral theme of existing upholstery fabrics, wallpapers or carpets, or introduce a touch of femininity to neutral, non-flowery decor.

You can display several identical cushions, alternate two patterns, or build up a free-for-all display, perhaps based on a broad colour theme or one type of flower. You can make or buy all the cushions at once, for an instant effect, or enjoy adding to the collection gradually.

If you are making your own cushions, printed fabrics are ideal for quick results, but if you have the time and patience, you can appliqué floral cutouts on to plain fabric; quilt and pad floral fabric or appliqués for a sculptural, three-dimensional look; or make embroidered or stencilled cushions. If you use different but toning floral-patterned fabric front and back, you can turn the cushion over when you feel like a change.

For a fragrant touch when making your own cushions, include a little pot-pourri or sprinkle a drop or two of essential oil, such as oil of lavender or oil of rose, in the padding.

These tulip-printed cushions, cut from extra curtain fabric, each contain a single unit of the diamond pattern. Plaid blue and white edging repeats the basic colour theme, with the striped cushions reflecting the soft greens and yellows that play a minor role.

▲ **For a formal effect**, display alternating patterns of floral cushions, upright and evenly spaced apart. Here, cushions made of the same airy chintz fabric as the sofa alternate with ones in a rich floral pattern.

▼ **A colourful display** of printed, patchwork and embroidered floral cushions transforms the feel of the slatted furniture in this garden room, lifting the impact of the dark paintwork with bold colour.

▶ **Like blue and white china**, mixed blue and white floral cushions have an endearing, enduring freshness. Here they add to the comfort of a white-painted wicker sofa, with two contrasting floral cushions as optional extras.

GUSSETED CUSHIONS

*Adding a gusset to feather cushions makes
them look deep and luxurious, and gives your foam
seat pads a professional, tailored finish.*

Gusseted cushions consist of a top and a bottom panel which are joined together with a strip of fabric known as a gusset. The result is a deep, plump, and tailored looking cushion, which has a range of uses from sofa cushions to window seat padding and comfy footstools. Emphasize the three-dimensional shape with piped or corded seams, or make the gusset itself in a contrasting colour or fabric.

You can use feather or synthetic cushion pads, or for a firmly moulded cushion, deep foam. The easiest way to put the pad inside the cover is to leave one side seam open, insert the

pad, and then slipstitch it together by hand. However, you need to unpick and restitch the seam each time the cover is cleaned, so for ease, insert a zip opening.

If your cushion pad is soft, the opening need only be the same size as one side of the cushion; if it is slightly more rigid, like a foam pad, the opening needs to extend 10cm (4in) around each back corner, so you can remove the pad easily. Take this into account when measuring up and cutting out your fabric, and buy a zip that is 20cm (8in) longer than the back measurement of the pad.

A deep gusseted cushion is the best choice for adding comfort to a firm chair. Here the line of the gusset is emphasized by changing the direction of the stripes, while the piped edge serves to define the generous shape of the cushion.

MAKING THE COVER

For a hard wearing, practical cover use a firmly woven medium to heavyweight fabric – strong furnishing cottons are ideal. Alternatively, upholstery fabrics such as velvet give a good result, though they are a little more difficult to handle. Measure the chair seat and buy a pad or have a block of foam cut to these measurements. The instructions given here show a cover with the gusset made in two sections, a strip for the front and sides, and a back strip which extends round to each side and has the zip fastening.

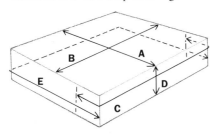

1 Measuring and cutting
Measure the pad and cut two panels, each as wide (**A**) and as long (**B**) as the pad, adding 1.5cm (⅝in) all round for seams.
For the back gusset, cut a strip the length of the zip (**C**) plus 3cm (1¼in), and as wide as the pad is deep (**D**) plus 6cm (2½in).
For the front gusset, cut a piece of fabric as wide as the depth (**D**) and as long as the total length (**E**) of front and sides, adding 1.5cm (⅝in) all round for seam allowances.

4 Attaching piping (optional)
Make two strips of piping each the same length as the finished gusset plus 2.5cm (1in) for overlaps. With raw edges even, tack piping to right side of top and bottom panels of cushion cover. For neat corners, clip into piping seam allowance at corners.

5 Attaching gusset to base With right sides together and centring zip around back of cushion, pin gusset to base. Starting 2.5cm (1in) from raw short edge, stitch gusset in place. Stop 7.5cm (3in) from starting stitches. For neat corners, stitch to corner and, with needle in fabric, raise the presser foot. Pivot fabric, lower presser foot, continue stitching. Snip corners.

6 Joining gusset Adjust unsewn edges of gusseted panel so that the length of the gusset, when sewn, will fit the bottom cushion panel. Pin in place and stitch gusset ends together, catching in ends of zip tape at same time. Trim excess fabric and press seam open. Complete stitching gusset to base.

A separate gusseted cushion adds extra comfort to this upholstered chair. For cushions with rounded corners, you should cut out shaped top and bottom fabric panels using the cushion pad as a guide.

2 Inserting the zip Cut back gusset in half lengthways. With right sides together, tack a 1.5cm (⅝in) seam and press it open. Place the zip face down on the wrong side, pin and then tack. Stitch into place from the right side.

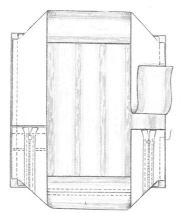

3 Joining the gusset strips
Press under 5cm (2in) on one short end of front gusset. With right sides up and side edges aligned, position front gusset over back covering zip tab. Topstitch through all layers at base of zip and again along folded edge to within 2cm (¾in) of each side of zip.

gusset

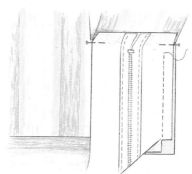

7 Attaching top panel
Fold gusset at corners and mark corners on the unstitched edge with pins. With zip open and right sides together, pin tack and stitch gusset to top panel, aligning corners. Clip into allowance at corners. Turn cover to right side and ease it into shape. Insert pad.

ROUND GUSSETED CUSHIONS

*Round gusseted cushions make an interesting change to the
angular square variety and, as they are not widely available ready-made,
are a very worthwhile home sewing project.*

Round cushions with a piped trim and buttoned centre look appealing on their own or among a pile of cushions of all shapes and sizes. Filled with a soft feather or foam pad they provide welcome padding on a bare seat or additional support on an upholstered chair. The extra depth of a gusset panel sewn between the back and front of the cover allows for a more substantial pad, giving the cushion added body and comfort.

The gusset strip is divided into two sections – the main gusset, extending two-thirds of the way around the cover, and a zip gusset that covers the remaining third. The zip gusset has a centred opening along its length that is wide enough for the cushion pad to fit through. A zip fastener at the opening makes the cover easy to remove for washing; its position within the gusset means the cover looks good from both the front and back.

As for other cushion types, choose your fabric with the rest of your furnishings in mind. A tightly woven, hardwearing fabric that washes well is ideal. Alternatively you can use an upholstery fabric but make sure it is not too heavyweight or you may find it difficult to work with.

A deep, round cushion adds a softening touch to the geometric lines and firmly upholstered appearance of this sofa.

MAKING A ROUND GUSSETED CUSHION

The zip gusset on this cushion is one-third the length of the entire gusset, so that whatever size your cushion is, you can slip the pad in and out of the cover easily. Measure the circumference of the cushion pad and then divide by three to find the length of the zip you need.

YOU WILL NEED

- ❖ ROUND CUSHION PAD
- ❖ TAPE MEASURE
- ❖ PATTERN PAPER
- ❖ DRAWING PIN AND STRING
- ❖ FURNISHING FABRIC
- ❖ ZIP AND TWO SELF-COVER BUTTONS
- ❖ MATCHING THREAD
- ❖ PIPING CORD AND ZIP FOOT (optional)

1 Cutting the circular panels
Measure the cushion pad radius (**A**). Fold a square of paper, a bit larger than the pad, into quarters. Tie a length of string to a drawing pin and pin it through the folded corner of the paper to a cutting surface. Tie the opposite end to a pencil so the taut string measures **A**. Holding the pencil upright and the string taut, draw an arc across the paper. Cut along the arc and unfold the paper. Centring any motifs, pin this pattern to the right side of the fabric. Adding a 1.5cm (⅝in) seam allowance all round, cut out two circles of fabric.

2 Cutting out the gussets
For the main gusset, measure the depth (**B**) and two-thirds of the circumference (**C**) of the cushion pad. Adding a 1.5cm (⅝in) seam allowance all round, cut a strip of fabric to this size.
For the zip gusset, measure one-third of the circumference (**D**) of the cushion pad. Add 6cm (2¼in) to **B** and 3cm (1¼in) to **D** for seam allowances, and cut a strip of fabric to these measurements. Fold the zip gusset piece in half lengthways and cut along the fold line to form two zip gusset pieces.

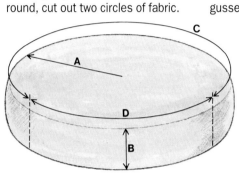

◪ *A piped trim around the rim and a fat covered button at the centre exaggerate the curvaceous look of this round gusseted cushion.*

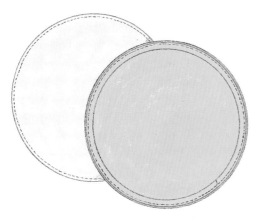

3 **Adding piping (optional)** Measure the circumference of one of the circular panels. Using the main fabric or a contrasting fabric, make two strips of covered piping, the length of the cushion pad circumference plus 2.5cm (1in) for overlaps. With the right sides together and matching the raw edges, pin the covered piping all round the front and back circular panels. Tack the piping in place, neatly overlapping the ends and snipping into the edges as necessary for ease.

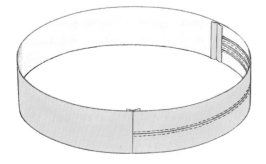

4 **Inserting the zip** With right sides together pin and tack the zip gusset pieces together along one long edge. Press the seam open. Pin and tack a zip, the same length as the zip gusset, face down along the wrong side of the seam. Working from the right side, stitch the zip in place. With right sides together stitch the short edges of the zip gusset to the short edges of the main gusset. Press the seams open.

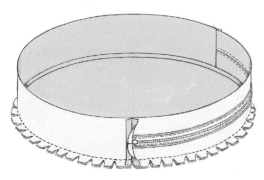

5 **Stitching the cover** With right sides together, pin and stitch one edge of the gusset around the front panel, using a zip foot if you are piping the cushion. Make snips into the seam allowance to help the gusset lie flat. Open the zip, then stitch the other edge of the gusset to the back panel.

6 **Completing the cover** Neaten the seams and turn the cover right side out through the zip opening. Insert the cushion pad and close the zip. Stitch two covered buttons to either side of the cushion (optional).

▲ *Florals and stripes always strike up happy relationships. Here a red-and-white striped gusset is paired with a traditional, rose-patterned fabric on the front panel of a round cushion.*

113

MAKING A PLEATED GUSSETED CUSHION

This gusseted cushion cover has circular pleated panels at the front and back which you make by folding a strip of fabric into a large rosette. To hide the stitching in the centre of the pleating you can trim the panels with a miniature rosette and assemble the cover in exactly the same way as a plain round gusseted version. Apart from a remnant of fabric for the mini rosettes and tailors' chalk, you need the same materials as for *Making a Round Gusseted Cushion.*

1 Cutting the front and back panels Measure the circumference of the cushion pad (**A**) and the radius (**B**). Add 3cm (1¼in) to both measurements for seam allowances and cut two rectangles of fabric to this size.

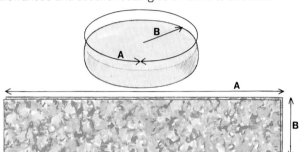

2 Preparing the panels Press and stitch a 1cm (⅜in) hem along one long edge of each rectangle. Fold the rectangles in half widthways with right sides together. Pin and stitch a 1.5cm (⅝in) seam along the short edges. Press the seams open and turn right side out. Using a tape measure and chalk, starting at the seam, mark the right side of each hemmed edge into sections about 5cm (2in) wide.

3 Pleating the panels On each ring of fabric match up the marks along the hemmed edge to form tight pleats. Finger press the pleats, allowing them to fan out along their length, and pin in place. Continue pleating the ring of fabric until it forms a flat pleated circle like a rosette. Check the pleats are even all round and adjust them if necessary. Using strong thread handstitch the pleats firmly together at the centre.

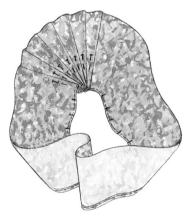

The front and back panels of these distinctive round gusseted cushions are made from neatly pleated rosettes of fabric. They are further embellished with contrasting buttons on central rosettes and rich golden cord.

4 Making the rosettes Cut two pieces of fabric measuring 20 x 10cm (8 x 4in). Following step 3 for pleating the front and back panels, make two miniature pleated rosettes from the fabric pieces, marking 2cm (¾in) wide pleats. Stitch a rosette to the centre of the front and back panels to hide the pleat stitches.

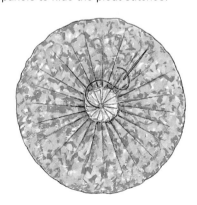

5 Assembling the cover Following steps 2-6, *Making a Round Gusseted Cushion*, make up the cushion cover, attaching piping around the edge of the front and back panels if you wish, and finishing with covered buttons at the centre of the rosettes.

LOOSE CHAIR COVERS

Give armchairs and sofas of all shapes and sizes a new lease on life with a fitted loose cover (slip cover) — they look great and they're easy to make.

S ofas and armchairs are often the main items of furniture in your living room, and an important and expensive purchase. So, when it comes to updating a room, you may have to keep your existing sofa, even if it does not fit in with your new scheme. By making your own loose covers, however, you can create a completely fresh look to fit in with your room's new image and keep within budget.

Professional-looking loose covers are surprisingly simple to make. If you already have a loose cover, you can use that as the pattern. Otherwise, you need to measure the chair or sofa carefully, then make a rough pattern from calico or an old sheet.

Piece the fabric panels together and pin them in place on the armchair, then adjust and trim them to fit. A fastened opening at the back makes the cover easy to take on and off, and lets you remove it for washing.

Choose fabrics that are hardwearing, firmly woven, crease resistant and washable. Avoid heavy fabrics as they are difficult to stitch, especially if you'd like piped seams. It is easiest to work with plain or all over patterned fabrics so you do not have to match the pattern or centre the motifs. Make sure when working with stripes or checks that the lines in the pattern align vertically and horizontally, and match at obvious places such as the front of the arm.

A new loose cover instantly spruces up a comfortable but unattractive sofa and, since it is removable and washable, it is a really practical option for family rooms.

MAKING LOOSE COVERS

The instructions given here are for a box shaped sofa. To cover a sofa or chair with curved or shaped arms, refer to *Covering a Rounded Chair* on page 118.

Before covering the sofa, check the underlying upholstery is in good condition, so you can be sure the covers will fit smoothly. Add padding to cushions if you want to make them plumper, and make repairs to the lining fabric with a few stitches or by sewing a patch.

It helps to decide on the positions of the seamlines and then measure all the chair dimensions from the widest points of each panel. Make a scale pattern to estimate fabric. For more details, see pages 119-120.

Make a rough pattern from calico or an old sheet. Since the covers tuck in round the seat, you need to add a tuck-in allowance of 15cm (6in) along the inside edges of the inner seat panels. The procedure for measuring up a chair or sofa of a similar style is identical.

Approximate fabric requirements

Chair or sofa	Fabric needed/m (yd)
Armchair	5.5-7m (6-7½yd)
Two-seater sofa	7-9m (7½ -10yd)
Three-seater sofa	10-13m (11-14¼yd)

MAKING THE PATTERN

1 Measuring up Remove cushions and loose covers. Measure each panel of the sofa across its widest point and note the dimensions. Add 5cm (2in) to each measurement for 2.5cm (1in) seam and hem allowances. Add 15cm (6in) tuck-in allowances along edges of inside back (**A**), inside arm (**C**) and seat (**E**) pieces.

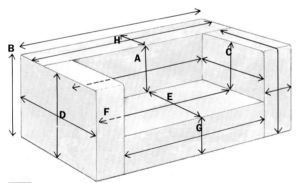

4 Assembling the arms Position **D** in place, pinning the back edge to panel **B**. Position **C** in place, so the tuck-in allowance runs along the seat at the base and lower edge. Pin the back edge of **C** to the sides of **A**. Pin the arm gusset (**F**) to **C**, **D** and **H**.

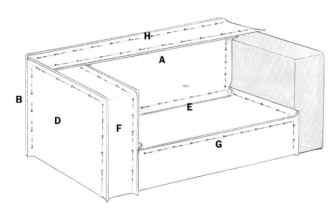

2 Cutting the calico pattern Cut a rectangle of calico for each sofa panel to the measurements taken. Cut one set of arm panels pattern pieces and reverse for other arm.

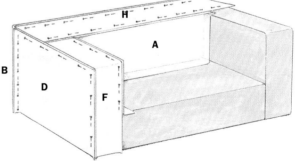

3 Assembling the back pieces Position the panels **A** and **B** on the sofa, with the tuck-in allowance for **A** along the lower edge. Pin the centre of each panel to the sofa then, smoothing fabric taut, pin it to the edges of the sofa. Pin gusset (**H**) along the upper edges of **A** and **B**.

5 Assembling the seat and front Pin the seat (**E**) to **A** and **C**, with the tuck-in allowances at the back and sides. Pin the front gusset (**G**) to **E** and **F**. With chalk, mark the seamlines around the edge of the chair on the pattern pieces, adding tuck-in allowances where necessary.

6 Trimming the pattern Remove the pattern pieces one at a time and mark them with their name and pattern or grain direction. The grain should run vertically or from front to back when the fabric is on the chair. Trim the pattern pieces to shape, remembering that you've added a 2.5cm (1in) seam allowance around each piece, and a 5cm (2in) hem allowance to the lower edge of pieces **B**, **D**, **F** and **G**.

MAKING UP THE COVER

1 Cutting out Note: you may have to join fabric for large pattern pieces. Lay out the pattern pieces on the fabric, following the grain. If using patterned fabric adjust positions so patterns match. Reverse the arm pieces for left and right arm. Cut out fabric pieces, joining widths if necessary.

2 Pinning cover With wrong sides up, reassemble the cover pieces on the sofa following the same sequence as the pattern pieces. Ease the tuck-ins into place to check their fit around the seat. Mark fabric seamlines with chalk all round the edges of the sofa, adding tuck-in allowances. Fit a zip, to open upwards, at the left side of the outside back panel.

3 Adding piping (optional) Cut piping from excess cover fabric or a contrast fabric. Before tacking cover pieces together, insert the piping between the seams. Taper piping into the seam where the piped seams cross.

4 Tacking cover Remove the cover and tack it together, following the pinning order. Turn cover to right side and place over the sofa to double check the fit. Adjust the seams if need be. Turn to wrong side and stitch seams together. Zigzag stitch raw edges to neaten.

5 Hemming cover Turn up and stitch a 2.5cm (1in) double hem all round the lower edge of the cover, mitring the corners at the bottom of the zip to neaten.

6 Making cushions Measure and make up the cushion covers following instructions for gusseted cushions on page 110.

7 Adding cushion bows (optional) Cut two bow strips for each cushion, 100cm (39½in) long and 12cm (4¾in) wide. Fold strips in half lengthways with right sides together. Stitch ends and long edge, leaving a 5cm (2in) gap for turning. Turn to right side, press and slipstitch gap closed. Tie strips into bows and handstitch to the front of the cushion covers.

◣ A sofa takes on a completely fresh look with a brand new loose cover in crisp blue stripes and coordinating gingham ribbons.

COVERING A ROUNDED CHAIR

The technique for covering a sofa or chair with rounded contours is essentially the same as for a box shaped sofa and uses the same materials. However, with this style it is especially important to make a pattern to ensure that all the rounded seams of the final cover fit smoothly.

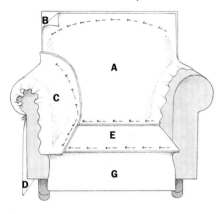

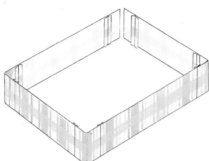

5 Sewing the skirt With right sides together, pin and stitch skirt and pleat inserts into a long strip, taking 2cm (¾in) seams. Begin and end strip with a half insert and place the other inserts between skirt panels. Press under and stitch a double 1cm (⅜in) hem along lower and side edges.

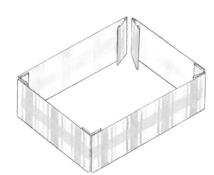

6 Adding the skirt Matching right sides, bring the seamlines together to pleat up insert. Pin and tack pleats at raw edges. With right sides together and raw edges even, pin the skirt to the lower edge of the loose cover so the half inserts are at the bottom of the zip, matching pleats to chair corners. Tack and stitch together, neatening raw edges with zigzag stitch. Stitch hooks and eyes to fasten edge at base of zip.

1 Cutting pattern Measure the chair and cut out calico rectangles following steps 1–2 on the previous page, omitting the top back gusset (**H**). Cut a separate front panel **F**, and take **C** round to cover the top of the arm.

2 Assembling the pieces Position **A** and **B** on the chair and pin them together across top of chair back. Pin **E** to lower edge of **A** allowing for tuck-in at seat back. Pin the front gusset **G** to **E**. Pin **C** to **A** and **E** allowing for tuck-ins. Shape the back corner tuck-in to a point. Pin **D** to **C** and **B** so arm seam lies under scroll. Pin **F** in place and draw shape of gusset.

3 Sewing cover Trim the pattern and make up the fabric cover following steps 3-4 on previous page. It may be necessary to take out some of the fabric fullness around curves with small, evenly placed darts at the seams. Clip into seam allowance round curves.

4 Cutting out skirt Fit the cover over the chair. Mark a chalk line all round the lower edge of the cover at the desired height of the skirt. Measure length of each side of the cover at the chalk line, adding 4cm (1½in) to each side for seams. Cut four skirt panels to this size by the required height, plus 3.5cm (1⅜in) for hem and seam. Cut four square pleat inserts, with sides equal to the skirt depth. Cut one pleat insert in half.

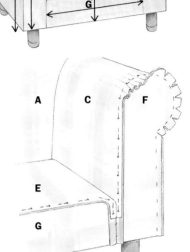

◪ *A loose cover in bright contemporary checks rejuvenates an armchair. Piped seams and a pleated skirt are simple to add and give a really professional look.*

118

Measuring up sofas and chairs

For successful loose covers, the planning and cutting of the pattern is vital, but first you must measure up your chairs accurately.

Well-fitting loose covers are a practical alternative to fixed upholstery for covering sofas and chairs. They provide an economical way of updating a room scheme or revitalizing worn furniture, and you can even create a coordinated set from a previously mismatched collection of chairs.

To estimate how much fabric you need, you have to measure all the dimensions of the chair and draw up a scaled pattern layout. To make sure that the actual loose cover fits neatly, these measurements help you to cut a rough pattern from an old sheet or piece of calico. You then piece the pattern together on the chair, adjust and trim it to fit and use it as a template for the actual fabric pieces.

Loose covers are not difficult to make, but it is a good idea to master the basic techniques by starting with a plain fabric or an all over pattern.

Planning

Before measuring the chair decide on the style of the cover – whether you want it to have a skirt (valance), or if it is to be piped. Arrange the position of the seams and openings so that it's easy to add appropriate hem and seam allowances in the correct places.

Seams

Plan the position of the seams, following the outlines of the chair and measure each panel between planned seamlines. If possible, avoid unnecessary seams by cutting the seat and front gusset in one, for example.

Fastened openings

In order to fit the cover over the chair an opening is usually left along one side edge of the outside back panel and a fastening fitted. Alternatively, you can make a feature of seams by positioning them at the front and fastening them with ties or buttons.

Joining widths

If you have to join widths of fabric for the inner back, seat and front gusset, place one width of fabric in the middle and join strips, selvedge to selvedge on either side, taking care to match patterns.

Alternatively, line the seams up with the edges of the seat cushions or down the centre of the sofa. With plain fabric you may be able to avoid joining widths by using the fabric sideways.

For a gusset that runs along the back and arms of a chair, you may need to join lengths. Where possible, position seams at the corner angles.

TIP
OLD COVERS

If you are replacing an old armchair or sofa cover, you can take it apart and use it as the pattern. However, make sure that the old cover fitted the chair or sofa correctly and that you patch up any gaping holes or jagged tears, otherwise the pattern may end up out of shape.

Measuring up

There are general rules that apply to measuring all types of chairs and sofas, which can be adapted to suit specific styles. But before you start, remove cushions and old loose covers.

❖ Measure each chair panel, widthways and lengthways, across the widest point, and list the dimensions.
A   inside back (add tuck-in allowance to lower edge)
B   outside back
C   inside arm (add tuck-in allowance to lower and back edges)
D   outside arm
E   seat (add tuck-in allowance to back and side edges)
F   arm gusset
G   front seat gusset
H   top back gusset strip

❖ **Seam allowance** Add 5cm (2in) to each measurement for 2.5cm (1in) seam allowance. This allows for some adjustment when you stitch the cover together – you can always trim away the excess seam allowance after you've joined the panels.

❖ **Tuck-in allowance** To anchor the cover in place, add a tuck-in allowance round the inner panel edges which you push down around the seat. Add 15cm (6in) tuck-in allowance to lower edge **A**, lower and back edges **C**, and back and side edges **E**.

❖ **Lower hem allowance** If you don't want a skirt with your cover, you can use a cased drawstring to hold the lower edge of the cover in place underneath the chair. Add a 20cm (8in) turning to the lower edge of pieces **B, D, F** and **G**.

Including a skirt or valance

If you decide to have a skirt (valance) round the base of the chair, shorten the length of pieces **B**, **D**, **F** and **G** by the depth of the valance and add a seam allowance rather than a hem allowance to each lower edge.

There are various styles of valance – adjust the measurements according to the style you want. Draw a horizontal chalk line round the chair at the desired height of the valance and measure – this is the length you must alter. For the depth of fabric, measure from the line to 1cm (⅜in) off the ground, add 1.5cm (⅝in) for the top seam and 5cm (2in) for a double hem.
Flat valance – add 5cm (2in) for a double hem at short edges.
Gathered valance – multiply by 1½ or 2.
Box pleated valance – multiply by 3, plus 1.5cm (⅝in) for seam allowances and 5cm (2in) for a double hem at either short edge.
Mock corner pleats – add 4cm (1½in) for side hems at each corner and 80cm (31½in) for corner backing panels.

Measuring up other shapes

Scrolled backs or arms Make sure that the inside back (**A**) or inside arm (**C**) wraps round the top of the curve, ensuring the seam lies at the bottom of the scrolled arm or back.

Shaped arm gussets Cut a rectangle of pattern fabric to measurements (**F**) and pin to the front of the arm. Draw the shape of the arm, add a 2.5cm (1in) seam allowance all round and cut it out. Recheck the fit.

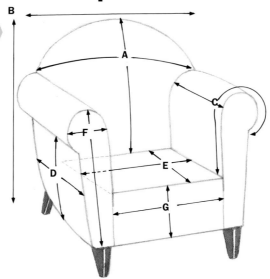

Winged chairs Measure **A** to include the inside of the wings on either side, allowing 5cm (2in) for tucking into the inside back creases. Then take additional measurements for the outside of the wing (**I**), and the wing gusset if you need to, adding seam allowances all round.

Armless chair Measure the inside back (**A**), outside back (**B**) and seat (**E**) in the usual way. Then measure the side seat gusset (**J**) all round the seat base.

Estimating fabric amount

To estimate how much fabric you need, draw up scale plans of all your pattern pieces and use them. With large motif patterns such as the floral illustrated, also mark the length of the pattern repeat and the positions of the main motifs on your scale drawing, so you can centre the motifs on the main chair panels and match the pattern across the seams. Small scale patterns do not need to be matched.

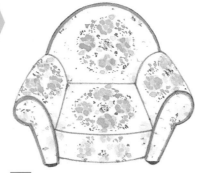

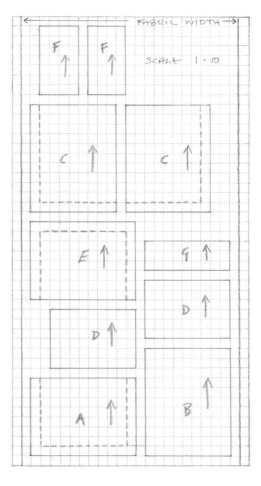

1 **Scale drawing** Using a scale of 1:10, draw the pattern pieces on graph paper. Label, mark direction of fabric grain and pattern with an arrow and cut them out. On a second sheet of graph paper, mark the fabric width to the same scale.

2 **Placing pieces** Mark pattern repeats and positions of large motifs on the second piece, and fit cut-outs on it, following the direction of the grain. Place large motifs centrally in main panels and match across seams. Multiply the length of graph paper layout by 10 to work out how much fabric you need.

Fresh and dried flowers and Victorian china are combined in this carefully composed display, based on pale pink and milky white. Chrysanthemums and pot-pourri feature in the fireplace, while spray carnations and mixed dried flowers add cheer to the mantelpiece.

FLOWERS IN FIREPLACES

As well as housing cosy flames in winter, fireplaces can provide a dramatic setting for displays of cut flowers in warm weather or, in the case of a disused fireplace, all year round.

Fireplaces form the natural focal point of many living rooms, dining rooms and even some bedrooms, reflecting their original role as the main source of domestic heat. Today, with almost universal central heating, many fireplaces remain unused – but you can still make use of their eye-catching properties by filling them with cut flowers.

The black grate makes a stark theatrical backdrop for a seasonal floral display, and the mantelpiece above offers another home for a smaller, complementary version of the main arrangement.

Try to keep the display in scale with the setting – tiny arrangements on their own are liable to look isolated and lost. Don't be afraid to use accessories – collections of china, ornaments, seashells, water-washed stones or pretty baskets – to add volume to a smaller display. Pictures of flowers or foliage hung over the mantelpiece add a gentle, pleasant confusion between two and three dimensional flowers and, at the same time, add visual impact to a modest display of cut flowers.

Don't ignore the style of the surround, whether stripped-down modern, country pine, Art Deco, Victorian or Classical. Carefully choose the container, the flowers, their arrangement and the accessories to set off the fireplace and surround.

▲ Informal bunches of roses, hydrangeas, ranunculus and laurustinus – large for the fireplace, smaller for the mantelpiece – enhance the delicate, shell pink dish and elegant Regency fireplace, decorated with a scallop-shell motif.

▶ A wrought-iron fire basket filled with pine cones forms the base for a wicker basket of lilies, tulips, stocks and delicate blossom. Carefully placed sprigs of purple statice add colour to an otherwise all-white display.

◀ Humorous and light-hearted, a tulip and eucalyptus filled metal bucket is set against an ornate fireplace surround. Tulips and bear grass on the mantelpiece add a three-dimensional touch to the photographs of ferns and ivy.

▲ An informal posy of cornflowers, poppies and daisies adds a cheerful, summery touch to this modern, narrow brick fireplace. The trio of earthenware jugs blend well with the bricks and quarry tiles, reflecting their similar origins.

EVERLASTING ROSE TREE

*For an eye-catching centrepiece or mantel decoration,
you can transform a simple bunch of dried roses into an elegant
and long-lasting flower tree.*

Easily and quickly made, a flower tree can be decorated with almost any small dried flowers that have sturdy stems. Here, wine-red roses were used to top two stems of twisted twigs, but a single twig or a straight bamboo cane could be used instead. Quick-drying cement in a terracotta pot holds the stems in place and provides stability, while a florist's foam ball gives shape to the tree. As a finishing touch, dried reindeer moss, tucked around the base, looks pretty and hides the cement. An old-style terracotta pot goes particularly well with this sort of arrangement, but as wet cement stains, keep it well away from the outside and the rim of the pot. Alternatively, use a plainer pot and stand it in a decorative container to match your room.

*A bunch of
dried flowers
can easily be
transformed
into an elegant
38cm (15in)
tall tree.*

MAKING THE ROSE TREE

YOU WILL NEED

(for red arrangement on previous page)

❖ TERRACOTTA FLOWERPOT, height and diameter 10cm (4in)

❖ ADHESIVE TAPE

❖ PLASTIC BAG to line pot

❖ Small bag of QUICK-DRYING CEMENT

❖ Two twisted TWIGS from the garden, or a 27cm (11in) length of BAMBOO CANE, up to 2.5cm (1in) in diameter

❖ FLORIST'S DRIED FLOWER FOAM BALL, 10cm (4in) diameter

❖ 3 dozen DRIED ROSEBUDS for 38cm (15in) tree

❖ REINDEER MOSS

❖ FINE FLORIST'S WIRE

❖ CLEAR ADHESIVE

1 Preparing the pot Make the pot watertight by taping over the drainage hole on the inside and then lining the pot with plastic, trimming the plastic 2.5cm (1in) above the rim. Keeping the mixture fairly stiff, make up the quick-drying cement and fill the pot to within 2.5cm (1in) of the rim.

2 Securing the stem Push the twig stems into the centre of the pot, intertwining them if possible. Leave to set overnight, checking for the first hour or so that the stems are still upright. When the cement has set firm, trim away surplus plastic. Push the foam ball on to the top of the stems, making sure it stays central.

3 Adding roses Gently remove the dried rosebud leaves from the main stems, and trim the rosebud stems to 2.5cm (1in). Push the rosebuds into the foam ball, turning the pot as you work to create a good round shape and an even distribution of roses.

Smaller than the wine-red tree shown overleaf, this 25cm (10in) high flower tree in a 7cm (3in) pot is made in the same way. Here, an 18cm (7in) length of bamboo cane is used instead of twigs and the foam ball holding about 24 dried roses is 7cm (3in) in diameter.

4 Adding the leaves Bunch together two or three leaves and wind fine florist's wire around the stems. Trim the wire ends to 2.5cm (1in), twist together and push gently into the foam ball. Finally, fill any gaps with moss secured with hairpin-shaped wire loops.

TIP
MONEY SAVER
To keep down the cost of your flower tree, dry fresh roses yourself. After enjoying them as cut flowers, as soon as they start to wilt hang the roses upside-down in a cool, airy place for a week or so, until they are completely dry.

5 Finishing off Check the shape is symmetrical and pleasing, and make sure none of the foam ball is visible. Finally, tuck a cushion of moss around the base of the tree to hide the cement and the plastic, securing it with clear adhesive.

SILK FLOWER DISPLAY

Add a stylish touch to a quiet corner with this basket arrangement of silk flowers and foliage, and enjoy its enduring elegance long after the summer days are over.

Silk flowers are widely available these days and many are far less expensive than they used to be. Though there's no real substitute for the fresh beauty of real flowers, silk is a lovely natural material, and you can use silk flowers to create very pleasing displays. They are particularly useful when fresh flowers are in short supply and expensive; for those areas of the home where fresh flowers are short-lived – near a heat source, for example; or when caring for them is inconvenient and easily forgotten – perhaps when they stand in a guest bedroom or on a high shelf.

Another advantage of silk flowers, apart from their long life, is that you are not limited to a particular season. At any time of the year, you can enjoy the fresh yellows and blues of a spring display, the soft pastels or hotter colours of summer or the evocative autumnal hues of vibrant russet and gold.

As the silk flowers and foliage have wire stems, you can bend them gently to the desired shape. This makes it easy to achieve a soft, natural arrangement. You can tease individual petals or leaves into shape by holding the fabric between the thumb and the blade of a blunt knife. Pull the knife gently across the petal for a soft curl or apply more pressure for a pronounced curl.

This pretty basket arrangement uses soft peach roses and creamy white asters with red-tipped larkspur and dusky purple eucalyptus leaves to give a subtle blend of colour and texture. Preserved beech leaves blend well with the silk flowers, giving depth and lending a natural look to the design.

Silk flowers in delicate peach and creamy white are combined with dusky purple-grey and rich copper foliage. They coordinate well with the weathered-look basket.

MAKING THE ARRANGEMENT

Use dried florists' foam to hold the flowers in position. Remember that even if you place the display against a wall, you still see it from three sides, so insert the stems facing in different directions, pointing one or two slightly backwards to avoid a flat back to the design.

TIP

A SCENTED BOUQUET

Add a little rose- or lavender-scented pot-pourri to the container around the foam to give the display a delicately perfumed scent.

1 Preparing the container Wedge the dried florists' foam tightly into the basket, trimming if necessary to fit, to create a firm base for the display. Leave about 2.5cm (1in) of foam extending above the rim of the basket to carry some downward-sloping stems.

2 Preparing the silk flowers Using the scissors or wire cutters, cut the stems of the asters and roses to 18cm (7in) and the larkspur and eucalyptus to between 20-23cm (8-9in). Snip the copper beech stem into short 7.5cm (3in) lengths with a slanting cut.

3 Making the framework Insert the larkspur to form a framework for the display. Angle the side and front stems downwards over the basket edge. Place one or two stems in the centre facing forwards.

4 Adding the foliage Insert the short lengths of beech low down, fanning them out around the basket, so that they camouflage the florists' foam and give depth to the display.

5 Adding the roses Insert the roses, varying their heights, so that one or two are set quite close to the base to add interest.

6 Highlighting the display Add the asters between the roses, making sure that the flowers do not crowd each other. Position the eucalyptus stems to reinforce the spears of larkspur, creating textural interest. If necessary, fill gaps with more beech or eucalyptus.

USING PRESERVED FOLIAGE

Adding natural dried or preserved foliage to an arrangement gives a softer effect than silk leaves alone. You can preserve your own woody stems, such as beech, oak, eucalyptus and mahonia, by standing the split stems in 7.5cm (3in) of glycerine solution – one part glycerine to two parts hot water – and leaving them for two to three weeks until the solution is absorbed.

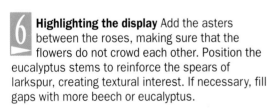

Index

ACKNOWLEDGEMENTS

Photographs

7 Habitat, 8-9(tl), 8(br) IPC Magazines/Robert Harding Syndication, 8(bl) The Image Bank, 9(tr) IPC Magazines/Robert Harding Syndication, 9(bl,br), 10(tl,tr,cr,br) The Image Bank, 10(cl) EWA/Michael Dunne, 11-16 Eaglemoss/Graham Rae, 17 EWA/Spike Powell, 18-19 IPC Magazines/Robert Harding Syndication, 20(cl) MFI, 20(bl) Jane Churchill, 20-21(t) MFI, 20-21(bc) Ariadne Holland, 20-21(br) IPC Magazines/Robert Harding Syndication, 22(tl) Sanderson, 22(tr) IPC Magazines/Robert Harding Syndication, 22(bl) EWA/Brian Harrison, 22(br) EWA/Spike Powell, 23, 24-25 IPC Magazines/Robert Harding Syndication, 26-27(tl) Laura Ashley, 26(b) EWA/Rodney Hyett, 27(tr,b) IPC Magazines/Robert Harding Syndication, 28(tl) Appalachia, 28(tr) Hill & Knowles, 28(c) IPC Magazines/Robert Harding Syndication, 28(bl,br) Appalachia, 29 Crown Paints, 30-31 Dulux, 32(t) IPC Magazines/Robert Harding Syndication, 32(b), 33(t) Ariadne Holland, 33(b) IPC Magazines/Robert Harding Syndication, 34(tl) Ikea, 34(tr) Eaglemoss/Graham Rae, 34 (bl, br) IPC Magazines/Robert Harding Syndication, 35 EWA/Brian Harrison, 36-37 Tintawn Carpets, 38 IPC Magazines/Robert Harding Syndication, 39(t) EWA/Peter Woloszynski, 39(bl) EWA/Michael Dunne, 39(br) IPC Magazines/Robert Harding Syndication, 40(t,cl,bl,br) Eaglemoss/Iain Bagwell, 40(cr), 41, 42-43 IPC Magazines/Robert Harding Syndication, 44(l) David Parmiter, 44(tr) IPC Magazines/Robert Harding Syndication, 44(br) EWA/Andreas von Einsiedel, 45(tr) Crowson Fabrics, 45(br) IPC Magazines/Robert Harding Syndication, 46(tl) Eaglemoss/Martin Norris, 46(tr) Kestrel, 46(cr) Marks & Spencer, 46(bl,br) Stag, 47 Habitat, 48-49 Laura Ashley, 50-51(t) David Parmiter, 50(b) IPC Magazines/Robert Harding Syndication, 51(tr) EWA/Spike Powell, 51(b) IPC Magazines/Robert Harding Syndication, 52(t) Habitat, 52(cl) Eaglemoss/Graham Rae, 52(bl,br), 53 IPC Magazines/Robert Harding Syndication, 54-55 Debenhams, 56-57(t), 56(c) IPC Magazines/Robert Harding Syndication, 56(b) Ariadne Holland, 57(tr) IPC Magazines/Robert Harding Syndication, 57(b) The Pier, 58(tl,br) Inspiration, 58(tr) Tomkinsons Carpets, 58(bl) Today Interiors, 58(bc) Eaglemoss/Steve Tanner, 59 IPC Magazines/Robert Harding Syndication, 60-61 Worldwide Syndication, 62-63(t), 62(bl) Ikea, 62-63(bc) Habitat, 63(br) PWA International, 64(tl,tr,c,bl) IPC Magazines/Robert Harding Syndication, 64(br) Eaglemoss/Graham Rae, 65 EWA/Graham Henderson, 66-67(t) Ikea, 66(bl) El Mueble, 67(br) EWA/Spike Powell, 68(t) Arcaid/Simon Kelly/Belle, 68(bl) Worldwide Syndication, 68(br) Doehet Zelf Holland, 69 EWA/Spike Powell, 70(cl) IPC Magazines/Robert Harding Syndication, 70(bl) Habitat, 70-71(br) EWA/Rodney Hyett, 71(t) MFI, 72(t) IPC Magazines/Robert Harding Syndication, 72(c) EWA/Rodney Hyett, 72(b), 73 Ikea, 74(t,b) Habitat, 74(c) Brights of Nettlebed, 75(t) Ikea, 75(b) Outline Upholstery, 76(t) Ikea, 76(b) Brights of Nettlebed, 77(t) Courts, 77(cl) Ducal, 77(b) Parker Knoll, 78 Marks & Spencer, 79 IPC Magazines/Robert Harding Syndication, 80(t) Worldwide Syndication, 80(b) Beaver & Tapley, 81(t) Hammel, 81(b) IPC Magazines/Robert Harding Syndication, 82-83(t) Mondadori Press, 82(bl) Ducal, 82(br) Hammel, 83(cr) Marks & Spencer 83(b) Ducal, 84(tr,br) Ikea, 84(c) Habitat, 85-87 Worldwide Syndication, 88(t) EWA/Rodney Hyett, 88(bl) Arcaid/Geoff Lung, 88(br) Worldwide Syndication, 89 Ikea, 90(t) EWA/Neil Lorimer, 90(bl) Christopher Wray's Lighting Emporium, 90(bc) EWA/Jerry Tubby, 90(br) Habitat, 91(t) Textra, 91(bl) Paul Ryan, 91(br) Christopher Wray's Lighting Emporium, 92(tl) Ikea, 92(tr,cr) Mazda, 92(bl) Habitat, 92(br) Ikea, 93-94 IPC Magazines/Robert Harding Syndication, 97 Eaglemoss/Simon Page-Ritchie, 98 Eaglemoss/Paul Bricknell, 99 Eaglemoss/Graham Rae, 100 Ariadne Holland, 101 The Pier, 102(t) IPC Magazines/Robert Harding Syndication, 102(cr) Fired Earth, 102(bl) Worldwide Syndication, 102(br) Eaglemoss/Steve Tanner, 103 Maison de Marie Claire/Chabaneix/Renault, 104(tl) EWA/Spike Powell, 104(cl,cr,bl) Marie Claire IdÇes/Schwartz/Chastres/Lancrenon, 104(r) Eaglemoss/Simon Page-Ritchie, 105, 106(tl) IPC Magazines/Robert Harding Syndication, 106(tr) Sanderson, 106(b) EWA/Andreas von Einsiedel, 107 Jane Churchill, 108(tl) EWA/Andreas von Einsiedel, 108(tr) EWA/Michael Dunne, 108(b) Ariadne Holland, 109 Harlequin Fabrics, 110 IPC Magazines/Robert Harding Syndication, 111 Sanderson, 112 IPC Magazines/Robert Harding Syndication, 113 Sanderson, 114 IPC Magazines/Robert Harding Syndication, 115 Ariadne Holland, 117 Marie Claire IdÇes, 118 Ariadne Holland, 121 EWA/Tom Leighton, 122(tl) Dulux, 122(tr, bl) IPC Magazines/Robert Harding Syndication, 122(br) Sue Atkinson, 123-124 Eaglemoss/Martin Chaffer, 125-126 Eaglemoss/Steve Tanner.

Illustrations

95-96 Terry Evans, 98-100 Sally Holmes, 110, 112-114, 116-118 John Hutchinson, 119-120 Terry Evans, 124 Christine Hart-Davies.